# EMBRACING ME

# EMBRACING ME

How 16 Women Found Their
Confidence To Shine

**Queens In Business**

# EMBRACING ME
## How 16 Women Found Their Confidence To Shine
© 2023 Queens In Business

All rights reserved. No part of this book may be reproduced, stored in a retrieval system or transmitted in any form or by any means (electronic, mechanical, photocopy, recording, scanning or other) except for brief quotations in critical reviews or articles, without the prior written permission of the publisher.

ISBN: 9798377772422 Paperback

Edited By: Sunna Coleman

Published By: Inspired By Publishing

Cover Designed By: Tanya Grant - The TNG Designs Group Limited

The strategies in this book are presented primarily for enjoyment and educational purposes. Every effort has been made to trace copyright holders and obtain their permission for the use of copyright material.

The information and resources provided in this book are based upon the authors' personal experiences. Any outcome, income statements or other results, are based on the authors' experiences and there is no guarantee that your experience will be the same. There is an inherent risk in any business enterprise or activity and there is no guarantee that you will have similar results as the author as a result of reading this book.

The author reserves the right to make changes and assumes no responsibility or liability whatsoever on behalf of any purchaser or reader of these materials.

# Acknowledgements

### By Sunna Coleman
Chief Editor and
Co-Founder of Queens In Business

Our confidence is shaped through many factors. From our earliest memories through to our life achievements and challenges, to our sense of self and who we surround ourselves with. Throughout my own life, my confidence has dipped, climbed, fallen, and eventually soared.

To get it to where it is today, I have four incredible women to thank, my fellow Co-Founders: Chloë Bisson, Carrie Griffiths, Shim Ravalia and Tanya Grant. These four inspiring entrepreneurs have shown me who I am capable of becoming and have helped me unlock my potential. I am forever grateful.

In this book, you will discover the powerful stories of sixteen female entrepreneurs and their own relationship with confidence. There will be stories you can relate to and stories you could never have imagined.

This book would not have been possible without the continuous talent and hard work of the publishing team, Angela Haynes-Ranger and Gaby Osias, as well as our Branding Queen, Tanya Grant who designs the stunning covers of all our books.

We hope you find strength and motivation in reading these stories. It is our mission to ignite confidence in as many female entrepreneurs as possible so that they can go on to make a real impact in whatever they choose.

## Dedication

This book is dedicated to women around the world who believed they didn't have a voice, realised that they did, and then had the confidence to use it.

With love,
Queens In Business

## Table of Contents

| | |
|---|---|
| Introduction | 1 |
| Embrace The Geek – Shim Ravalia | 3 |
| Break The Silence – Sunna Coleman | 12 |
| Show Up Like You're Meant To Be There – Chloë Bisson | 26 |
| Honestly Own It! – Tanya Grant | 38 |
| Stand Up And Claim What's Yours! – Carrie Griffiths | 50 |
| Never Too Late To Become Unstoppable! – Julie Fitzpatrick | 60 |
| Discrimination Won't Hold Me Back – Shelina Ratansi | 78 |
| Confident Leadership – Tess Cope | 90 |
| Reborn – Rajni Singh | 100 |
| Gem Made Under Pressure – Olufunmilola Olatunde | 116 |
| Counselling In Confidence – Jaimini Ravalia | 131 |
| Be Strong And Courageous – Olu Famakin | 148 |
| Return To Yourself – Christina Chalmers | 163 |
| The Storm To The Calm – Dr Irene Ching | 177 |
| You Are Not Broken – Dr Michelle Wyngaard | 191 |
| Getting Visible With Confidence – Paula Carnell | 208 |
| Conclusion | 214 |
| About Queens In Business | 215 |

# Introduction

Regardless of our path or journey through life, we all experience doubts, insecurities and, at times, the inability to believe in ourselves and our own self-worth. However, sometimes this can be based on the negative opinions and deeds of others which we find directed our way. We may look around us, and due to our circumstances, be left feeling hopeless and discouraged as what we see is not the path we had envisaged.

The people we trust and those we thought were there to love, protect and support us, are sometimes the ones who have a hand in giving us our greatest insecurities, chipping away slowly at our true selves, and leaving just a fragment of who we were behind.

In these times, it is easy to believe the narrative, easy to believe our lack of self-worth and feed into the feelings that we are less than, not good enough and not worthy, without the realisation that this is so far from the truth.

Sometimes, it takes a while to come to know and believe that we are everything we are meant to be and destined for so much more. If we're lucky, this comes early on, but sometimes it takes a while for us to challenge the storms, fight the battles and emerge on the other side, to then discover that we always had the warrior within us.

It's then that we begin to see and acknowledge our biggest growth. We realise the strength within us and are no longer willing to dance the dance to anyone else's tune but our own. We develop a feeling of self-assurance arising from an appreciation of our own special qualities and abilities and begin to believe that we can.

In this book you will find the incredible stories of 16 female entrepreneurs who have walked a journey which wasn't always easy. It was a journey of self-discovery, belief and determination leading them to be who they wanted to be. Their experience has made them into inspiring leaders with the ability to raise their voices and impact others around the world through their business and in their communities. We hope you will find strength in their words.

They have proved that what once seemed impossible, can indeed be possible.

# Embrace The Geek

### Shim Ravalia
Founder
The Gut Intuition

"Self-confidence is contagious"— Stephen Richards

Entrepreneurship is a language I always deep down believed in since I was knee-high to a grasshopper. It was something that I realised recently when my friend and business partner Carrie Griffiths shared something about her childhood that instantly opened up old memories for me.

As a little kid, I didn't play with Barbie dolls, in fact I loved playing with cars and riding my red, one-geared bike every day after school. I loved playing football, rounders, cricket, badminton, volleyball, table tennis, netball – anything that involved moving around, creativity, fun and made you think of little bits of strategy which brought out the rebellious and competitive streak in me that I absolutely LOVED.

Funnily enough, I loved creating and building a shop that sold absolutely everything from my bedroom to my parent's living room. I remember one Christmas in the early nineties, I begged my mum to get me my very own post office set. It was hilarious. I went with her to buy it and got really excited. She wrapped it in lovely Christmas wrapping which was even more exciting and then stood it against the Christmas tree because it was that big. I mean, as long as it was bigger and heavier than my brother's presents, I didn't care (competitive much?!).

Then came Christmas day and there it was, all shiny and ready to be ripped open! I still remember that feeling of opening it up and seeing it like it was the first time. I played post office for as long as I can remember, and I never got bored of it. I had my plastic coins, notes and stamps and took all my books, especially the Peter Rabbit collection which was the most expensive thing in my post office at the time, selling for a whopping two pounds. I loved selling to others and loved being sold to.

The only downside to running your shop in your living room is the lack of customers and forcing your family to buy something leaves you with a one-star review. This was just one of the "shops" I created through my childhood. I created many others such as an IT shop, clothes store, CD shop and many more. What I realised from this today is I am very clear and confident in how I serve others. I love creating money and spending it and I love creating something from scratch and building it up. This shows up in my life and my businesses today.

My very first business was called Fixed 4 Sport which I built from scratch having done the business plan at university for my Sports Business exam. I was excited to bring it to life and ran it for six years. The Gut Intuition was built from scratch in December 2019 and is still running well today and then came along Queens In Business in 2020, again built from scratch with five business partners to now a team of 13 people and growing.

The truth is, in all my business projects, I never doubted my abilities or confidence in making it work, I just knew it was going to work out because I believed in myself and nothing was going to get in the way of that.

Your childhood and what you loved playing as a kid can give you so many clues and ideas about you and your confidence and what you could possibly get involved in. I don't believe that as an adult you should ever forget what you were like as a child, there is just pure innocence and joy at that time that you can definitely bring into adulthood.

**The Kryptonite To Confidence**
I remember it being a Saturday afternoon and we had some relatives come over to visit us for a cup of tea. In Indian culture, it's very normal to discuss what your children are up to, what they are studying to be, what jobs they have… it's as if parents have a mental checklist ready to say out loud with pride of their children's achievements. It's almost an ego thing too – that energy of "my children are clever and they are doing better than yours and keeping the family name at the top". It seems to be okay to say. I write this while rolling my eyes!

As conversations were going on in the living room, I remember very clearly overhearing my dad saying that I would never amount to much with education. At the time, for a moment or two, I felt a bit crushed hearing that from my own dad, however, I chose not to react or believe what he thought was true for a second. I believe the kryptonite to confidence is listening to other people's opinion of you and what they think is best for you. Truth be told, no one knows other than you of your own true capabilities, your confidence and your clarity. If I listened to everyone's opinion of me, I certainly would not have achieved what I have achieved so far today, personally or professionally.

I did grow up experiencing a gender war that parents can often impose on their children. For me, I experienced on many levels throughout my childhood that boys in the family were always put on a pedestal to do great things like get a degree, be a doctor and make the parents proud because they are the ones that will carry the family name forward. On the other hand, girls were more favoured to get an education of some sort, find a husband, get married, have children and that's it. Being a curious child, I always asked my parents why this was the case and they never knew how to really give me a satisfying answer, it was always, "That's how it is done" or they just didn't know how to answer because they themselves didn't know the answer. Bringing curiosity into the mix can often help you with your confidence in asking better questions. The biggest question you should always ask yourself is, why?

Growing up, I often got labelled as a shy little girl. Sometimes, when I was around new people, there was a part of me that was shy but I felt that was quite natural being more of an introvert back then.

As years have gone by and I am in my mid 30s as I write this chapter, I wouldn't say I'm shy at all – more of an observer and an individual who really tunes into people's words as well as their energy and behaviours. I would say this is a true natural strength of mine that I have built up the confidence in sharing with others and bringing into my businesses when working with my partners and teams.

I would encourage you to be more curious about you and your personal development and come at it from an energy of discovery and wonderment. It's like a breath of fresh air learning about yourself and it's a never-ending rabbit hole. That's confidence that no one could ever take away from you.

**Behind The Geek, There's Always A Rebel**
Getting into my earlier years as a teenager, I was still that geeky little girl who never missed a day of school, did her homework, was the teacher's pet and a people pleaser. Back home, the environment was quite strict and suppressed and while as a kid it was okay, being a teenager, it was even worse.

There were many times I wanted to just speak up, scream at my parents and do what the hell I wanted to do. But the confidence just wasn't there because I feared my parents would be disappointed in me, and become even stricter. I have a very clear memory of when my parents found out that I got 13 out of 20 right in a spelling test. They both flipped out like it was the end of the world, coming home to my dad shouting out new strict rules of no more TV after school and study, study, study and more studying. There went my love for the Fresh Prince Of Bel Air on a Tuesday at 6pm.

I don't necessarily blame them for being this way when I was growing up because they had my best interests at heart of a good education and a good start in life which is something they both didn't have in their own childhood. However, suppression is a killer for confidence and even worse when other people just do it for you. My best advice here is don't be too strict on yourself or be rigid with your time and plans. Creativity and spontaneity really help your confidence levels come along.

My favourite memories of me being confident are when my rebellious side gave it a little helping hand in times of need and never left. As I entered Year 9 at secondary school, I decided to ditch the geeky look and just start being more me. My hair used to be down to my bum and I got it cut because it was a pain in the backside to maintain. My mother was not happy about it. I played more sports and hung out with the boys, I did drama after school for three years and I even bunked school for an afternoon too! Hardly rebellious, but it was for me at the time and it felt so liberating to expand my wings. I hung out with the "cool" people and some of them even became lifelong friends today.

I loved parents' evenings and pretty much all my teachers said to my mum that I was a very confident person and that I had a bright future ahead of me. If in doubt, dig out the old school reports and take a trip down memory lane. It's so nostalgic and heart warming to read through.

So being a rebel or rebellious does not necessarily mean getting in trouble with the law but you exercising that inner empress, your femininity to being your natural confident super power. It's the kind of feeling that you know what's good for you in that moment more than anything else.

Being a geek and rebel is the best combination that really does bring out the confidence you know you have in yourself.

Remember to appreciate and celebrate all aspects of you. For me, confidence is all about nurturing and celebrating the geek on one shoulder and the rebel on the other. Always listen to your intuition first because deep down you know what's best for you.

## About Me

I am the Founder of The Gut Intuition and COO for Queens In Business. I help business owners and entrepreneurs go from stress to unlimited energy and razor sharp focus without burning out in health and in business.

I've had the pleasure of being featured in many well known publications like Business Woman Today, CBS News, Fox, NBC and ABC to really spread my message and my vision about health for the future of entrepreneurs all over the world.

Born and bred in East London, and coming away from university with two degrees in Sports Rehabilitation, I worked in gyms and leisure centres until I found my entrepreneurial path.

Having been an entrepreneur for over 11 years now, I have overcome many hurdles and challenges with my own confidence. I hope that this book gives you the much needed boost to bring out that fiery confident person you know deep down you are and to continue rising above the noise no matter what.

# Break The Silence

## Sunna Coleman
Writing & Storytelling Coach
Writers Inspired

"Just like the lotus, we too have the ability to rise from the mud, bloom out of the darkness and radiate into the world" – Unknown

We all believe funny things when we're very little. We believe that if we make a silly expression and the wind blows, our faces will get stuck like that forever. We believe that our parents know the answers to everything. We believe that eating carrots gives us night vision, that monsters live under our beds, that reindeer can fly… What did you believe when you were a young child?

When our worlds are that small, almost anything we are told and that we encounter we take to be true. And the same can be said for our family life. Whether we have two parents, one or none, live with siblings or grandparents, have dinner at the table or on the sofa, brush our teeth before or after breakfast… Whatever we grow up with in those early years is what we take to be the norm.

It's not until we're able to communicate with other kids and reflect on our circumstances that we begin to realise that not everyone has the same experiences that we do.

I spent my earliest years growing up in Ilford, East London, the eldest child of two immigrant parents. When he was just ten years old, my dad escaped with his family from a spacious concrete house prone to unexpected break-ins from the local wildlife in Kampala, Uganda, to a small terraced house in the tidy streets of Wimbledon, London (thanks to Idi Amin). The first time he saw snow, he was so amazed that he didn't even feel the cold until other kids asked him where his jacket was!

My mum came to live with my dad in 1988, after getting married the year before during his trip to Lahore, Pakistan where she had grown up. The first time she saw snow she felt like she was on a beautiful movie set – having only seen it on screen before.

With my dad having spent the majority of his life in the UK and my mum having spent the majority of her life at the time in Pakistan, I had the influence of two cultures in my childhood. For the first six years of my life, this was my norm.

Ilford has a big South Asian community and the majority of my friends at school were of a similar background to me. Growing up in my little bubble, I was a very confident child with lots of friends, getting into trouble from time to time for chatting too much in class. I remember not having a care in the world and believing that I could be and do anything.

It wasn't until our family moved to Surrey in 1997 that my cosy little bubble suddenly burst.

**Different**

Running through the door to our new house for the very first time, I legged it upstairs to check out the bedrooms before my younger brother, Dan, could. The first was rectangular with pink floral wallpaper and white cupboards with pink trim that ran the whole way down one wall. The second bedroom was square with the same wallpaper but in blue. The last was a tiny box room that didn't capture my attention one bit. That could be saved for my brother.

So it was between the blue bedroom and the pink bedroom. "Can I choose my own room?" I shouted down to my parents who were moving the boxes in. "Yes!" my dad replied. Excellent.

The blue bedroom was situated at the front of the house and the pink one at the rear, overlooking the biggest garden I had ever seen. I decided I didn't want to be anywhere near the street as I was afraid of being close to the strangers outside. So the pink bedroom it was.

Moving home was so exciting as a six year old. It was such an adventure that I don't even remember missing any of my old friends that I had to leave behind – plus, I would have my *own* room for the first time! I felt so grown up and I looked forward to starting at my new school after summer.

Before I knew it, the first day of Year 2 had arrived. I put on my dark green sweatshirt over my light green checked summer dress, my knee-high white socks with my polished black boots (Mum always made sure our uniforms were pristine). I couldn't wait to meet my new class.

Sitting in the classroom while the teacher got ready to take the register, I felt nervous. The other kids were looking at me, wondering who I was. Most of them had been in school together since reception and knew each other. I was the new one. But not only that, most of them were White. Where were all the other Brown kids, I thought.

"Today we have three new pupils to welcome to the class," the teacher announced as everyone started looking around. I was relieved to hear that I wasn't the only one. "We have Catherine," the teacher said, "Christina, and Sunna." I felt immediately embarrassed as she pronounced my name wrong but I didn't want to speak up. I'd never encountered that before.

In that moment – being the only Brown kid in my class, being one of the only kids who didn't know the others, and having my name pronounced incorrectly – was the first time I started to feel like an outsider. In just a few minutes of my first day of school, I started to become acutely aware of my unfamiliar surroundings. I didn't know these people. They didn't know me. Was I strange to them?

Kids don't like to be different. They want to be accepted. To fit in. I went from a carefree and loud child to a very quiet one, taking in my new environment and noticing how the other kids spoke and acted, and what they discussed in the playground. It was completely alien to what I was used to. Looking back, I can see that I tried my best not to be noticed through my school years. I didn't want to draw attention to my "otherness." I wanted to look and act like everybody else.

I was afraid of bringing up references to my mixed culture because any time I had, I would be met with confused expressions and told that my family and I were weird. I don't blame the other kids. They didn't know any different from their bubble of reference either. The area that I lived in was predominantly White, so most people were not exposed to other cultures.

I did experience some bullying though in the form of name calling and racist remarks. Luckily I had the strength of character not to give them a reaction. But inside it hurt. It really hurt.

During the 90s and early 00s, the messaging in the media also exacerbated the problem. I don't remember ever seeing a woman of colour in magazines or advertising unless it was specifically to do with their culture – and even then, when it came to fashion, it would still be White models chosen to advertise the clothing. Being surrounded by this view in your society and in the media sends you a very strong message of what is considered "normal", "acceptable" and "desirable".

Before the move to Surrey, I used to love getting dressed up in colourful salwar kameez and lehengas at family parties. Since the move, I began rejecting that part of my identity, insisting I only felt comfortable in jeans. It wouldn't be until decades later that I made the sad realisation that I had changed from the core of who I was in an attempt to be accepted for so many years.

**Loss Of Innocence**
By the time I turned ten, I had started realising that things at home were not normal. I knew that everyone's parents disciplined them, some more than others, but I had not realised that what my family was experiencing was an extreme case.

My dad had anger issues and it would often be like dealing with Dr Jekyll and Mr Hyde. One minute, he'd be playful, encouraging us to run riot in the house. The next, he'd completely transform, his voice getting louder, his face stern, hands shaking and as kids, it seemed as though he got twice as tall.

When dad lost his temper, everyone had to tread very, *very* carefully. If you were not the subject of his anger, you could very easily become it with one wrong move. Suddenly, the house would descend into pure stillness and quietness. You would only speak if you were spoken to. And if you went against him, the situation would get worse for you and for everyone else. The scariest part was that it was unpredictable – anything could trigger him.

I remember going to Bluewater Shopping Centre with the whole family when I was around thirteen years old. Dan would have been around eleven and my sister, Zara, six. We were all in such a good mood, excited about what new clothes and toys we would buy. Mum, Zara and I went into Claire's. If you grew up in the UK around the same time as me, you'll remember how magical this store was for young girls. Every inch of the shop walls and floor were packed with fun, stylish (for the time) jewellery. I could spend hours in there.

My brother obviously had no interest so he waited outside with Dad. When we went shopping, Dad would often let Mum and I shop to our hearts' content, spending ages in every store while he and Dan sat outside or went to the boys' stores. On this day, however, he did not take it well. As we finally exited the store with all our goodies, a huge smile plastered across our faces, our stomachs lurched at the sight of Dad. He had 'the look' on his face. And we knew what that meant.

Confused as to why he was so angry today and had not been any other times we had spent ages in a shop, we tried to reason with him. We were out in public. We did not want to cause a scene. Why had he not just come inside and told us to hurry up, I thought. Whatever the reason, it was too late. The day was now ruined.

As punishment, Mum, Zara and I had to stand rooted to the spot with all our bags for hours while Dad took Dan to all the stores that he wanted to go and see. We were told that we were not allowed to move an inch – or else. I remember thinking that day how afraid my mum, a grown woman, must have been of the consequences to go along with this unfair punishment in public. She couldn't risk making it worse for her children.

While I went through a lot with my dad's anger issues, the worst moments were when I had to witness my brother or sister at the brunt of it. As the eldest, I felt an immense amount of protectiveness over them. If you're an older sibling, you can imagine how devastating it must have felt to watch them getting disciplined and not be able to say a word or show your emotion as they cower helplessly. My dad saw crying as a form of weakness. And if he spotted tears in your eyes, it would trigger him even more. Experiencing all of this made me grow up so fast.

Desperate to avoid any incidents, I would be on constant alert for the smallest of tell-tale signs that Dad was about to lose his temper. From his voice raising just a bit to his jaw clenching. It seemed to me that my mum wasn't able to pick up on these cues so well, and as the oldest child, I felt a responsibility to hold things together.

I'd try my best to settle any potential arguments before they erupted, communicating each person's side of the story in the way that they had meant it rather than how they were coming across. I'd plead with my brother and sister not to fight or cry or answer back in case they became the subject of his anger. I was jokingly given the nickname of "The Mediator" within my family. But to me it was no joke. It was survival.

It seems crazy to think that this was our reality for so many years. If you met him now, you would come to know a gentle giant. I am so proud of how he has improved – a victim of emotional and domestic abuse himself. His own father was much the same with him and his four younger siblings. And not only that, but his mother left the family when he was in his early twenties, leaving him to protect his younger siblings.

He grew up around violence, not only in the home but within 70s era London with White supremacist skinheads who would physically and verbally bully him. As I have grown older, I have come to understand where his anger issues stemmed from. I also learned that both of his parents had turbulent childhoods too. I am so grateful that the generational cycle is beginning to break.

Recently, my dad told me that the first time he realised he was having an impact on us was when I came to him after he had calmed down one time and I had spoken up about how it had made me feel. It is so important to be open about these experiences and learn from them rather than repress them and become what you once feared.

**Finding My Power**

Not being allowed to speak up or show too much emotion as a child meant that I turned to creative outlets to express myself. I loved to draw, paint and sing. As I entered my teenage years, I needed a more effective way to understand what I was feeling without speaking about it in the home. So I turned to writing.

Whenever I felt upset or angry after something had happened, I would write a song. I was drawn to lyrics and their hidden meanings. In song, you could write your truth without anyone really being able to tell what it's actually about. Only you knew what each word on the page was truly hiding.

It felt like such a release to get things out of my body and onto the page freely. In my everyday family life, I learned to be extremely careful with the language that I chose to use in case it triggered the wrong reaction. It meant that I found it really difficult to communicate what I wanted to say. I'd need time to think about what I should say and how I should say it before I allowed myself to convey it. I couldn't take the risk of getting it wrong. It put me under an immense amount of stress.

That's another reason I loved to write. You can take your words back by editing them if they're not exactly how you want your message to come across. Or you can rip up the piece of paper and throw it away so no one ever gets to hear what you said. I did this with a lot of my old writing from the most difficult times.

Writing and journaling hold a lot of power. They help you release, reflect, understand, learn and let go. Along with therapy, they are some of the most effective tools we can use to heal ourselves of our challenges and grow as people.

Without these tools, I would most likely have followed the same patterns and cycles that my family have gone through in their pasts. Instead, I have released and let go of my childhood hardship, not allowing it to hold me back any longer. Since doing so, I have noticed dramatic changes in how I feel and what I have been able to achieve. I understand myself better now, I feel at peace, I no longer feel afraid of voicing my truth. Sharing stories like these help stop the cycle and help others find a way out, knowing that they are not alone.

To me, this is what confidence is. The ability to share what's difficult and stand for what you believe in so that you can help others.

In the past, I was confused in my identity, hiding it and conforming to what I believed I needed to be. I was also afraid of voicing my opinion or acting in the wrong way. Now, I am comfortable with who I am and where I come from, and I am no longer afraid. When you feel comfortable, you exude confidence and that's what draws people to you and allows you to have a positive impact on others.

I've come a long way from the young girl who was afraid to be noticed. I have spoken on stages and been in multiple best-selling books. I've learned that it's okay to be unapologetically yourself. That repressing the real you can only lead to unhappiness. That if you don't speak up, then you can't inspire others to either. And that the world won't change if we aren't confident enough to release the ugly truth.

## About Me

I understand what it feels like to not be heard and to have your confidence shattered. Having gone through experiences in my childhood which silenced me, I turned to writing – my quiet way to release emotions and ask for help. That's why today, I'm passionate about helping female entrepreneurs express themselves with more confidence, using their past challenges to help break unhealthy cycles and positively impact thousands of lives.

I do this through my coaching programme, Writers Inspired. I believe that every voice matters and everyone has an inspiring message to share – even if you can't see it for yourself. I aim to share my message through my work, and to date, have been featured in multiple international #1 best-selling books, magazines, and on stages alongside the likes of the BBC, ITV, C4, CNN, Disney and Warner Brothers.

Great writing can help you leave a legacy and positively impact others for years to come. All you have to do is unlock your voice. It doesn't have to be perfect, it just has to connect.

I dedicate this chapter to my Queens In Business partners, Chloë Bisson, Carrie Griffiths, Shim Ravalia and Tanya Grant. Without these powerfully inspiring ladies, I would not have pushed myself half as hard as I have over the past few years. Through meeting them, I have transformed in confidence and have gone on my own healing journey in order to better help others. Love you all.

# Show Up Like You're Meant To Be There

## Chloë Bisson
Multiple Award-Winning Business Owner
Queens In Business

"The most beautiful thing you can wear is confidence" — Blake Lively

It was a Sunday morning. I woke up after a big night out and my head was pounding. I couldn't even lift my head off the pillow but my phone kept dinging. Before I had a chance to properly focus my vision, I saw a text message that was going to change my life forever.

That morning, whilst my boyfriend was downstairs making me breakfast, I found out that he was cheating on me. We'd been together for five years and we had just bought a four bedroom house. He had a great job that he'd been working towards for years and I had just been promoted in my job in the corporate world.

Life was great. Until it wasn't.

Before that morning, I would have said I was a pretty confident person. I was always the most talkative of the group, always organising our social events and making sure everyone was where they needed to be. In fact my parents would always say I was the 'bossy' one of the family.

But as soon as I found out the news on that Sunday morning, my confidence vanished in every aspect of my life.

I didn't trust him = How could he do this to me?
I didn't trust myself = How did I not see it coming?
I didn't trust my friends = How could they not tell me?
I didn't trust my thoughts = How will I get through this on my own?

Everything I'd known and believed was gone.


**Underneath The Confidence**
Nine years later and I've done a lot of work to get my confidence back, through counselling, therapy, journaling, meditation and many other techniques.

What stood out to me the most about this journey was that confidence isn't a personality type or something you're born with, confidence is a feeling that can come and go.

The dictionary definition is: the feeling or belief that one can have faith in or rely on someone or something.

So when we're talking about confidence, what we're actually talking about is the amount of belief and faith we have in ourselves.

Now for the raw and real part… How much do you believe in yourself right now? In fact, if you were to rate it on a scale of 1-10, how would you rate your belief in yourself?

For most female entrepreneurs, we're driven to create what we want but when it comes to having unwavering belief in ourselves, it can be difficult. Some might say because we've been told we can't do it or because others haven't believed us and therefore we learnt not to believe in ourselves.

But when you ask people that do have a strong belief in themselves, what is it that has created that strong belief, it often comes from an increased level of self-awareness and certainty in themselves and their strengths. And I believe that anyone can be confident and have a strong sense of self-belief if they have those two things: certainty and awareness.

For example, if I wanted to get more visibility by becoming a public speaker, my confidence would be based on the amount of *certainty* I have that I can actually do it and the *awareness* of how well I can do it. That's why people often think that practising something helps to build confidence because practice gives you the *certainty* that you can do it and *awareness* of how well you can do it.

So I believe instead of asking the question, "How can I be more confident?", the questions we need to ask are…

1. How can I be more certain and aware of myself?

2. What would need to happen for me to be certain I could do it?
3. If I was certain I could do it, how would I feel?

Because confidence really does start from within.

A really powerful exercise to build on your confidence is to write a list of all the things you're good at. Write a list of 50 things. Not 5… not 10… 50!

Start listing the things you can do well, your strengths, your abilities, your actions, your personality traits that serve you and anything else you can think of. Write as much as you can and if you get stuck, ask friends, family, even your followers, to share their thoughts.

Not only will you feel great when writing this list, becoming aware of all of your strengths, but this list will also act as a great reminder when you need it. If you're about to do something out of your comfort zone, read over the list and remember how great you are!

**Confidence In Being Visible**
Back in 2017 when I started my first business, I was extremely nervous about telling people. I had started to get my confidence back from my horrific breakup but being bold enough to shout from the rooftops about me starting my own business… that was a whole new level of vulnerability for me.

Yet sometimes we attract opportunities before we believe that we're actually ready for them.

A week after I started my business I woke up with a message on Facebook from a friend who was working at the local newspaper asking if she could interview me. I was speechless. She wants to interview me?!

Before I gave myself too long to think about it, I said 'yes'. After all, if I don't start getting known by people, how will I ever grow my business?

We met for coffee the next day and I was so nervous! I talked non-stop. I told her about my past, my business and my mission. I figured if I just kept talking through my nerves the interview would be over before I knew it.

And it was.

Before I had a chance to relax and be grateful it was over, she told me she had a friend that worked at our local BBC radio station that wanted to hear my story too. Holy sh*t.

A journalist asking me questions in a coffee shop to write in a newspaper is one thing but an interview on the radio where people will actually be listening… that was something else.

What do I need to prepare? What will she ask me? What will I say? What if she asks me a question I don't know the answer to? What do I wear?

"Chloë, it's a radio interview, no one will see what you're wearing," said Cedric, my supportive boyfriend, with a smile on his face. He was right. I was worrying so much because this time it would be live, another step out of my comfort zone. And that was when it dawned on me. That journalist who interviewed me and recommended me for BBC radio wouldn't have done it if she didn't believe in me and my message. So if she believed in me and thought I could do it then why not borrow her belief in me?

Because the truth is that most people only believe in their ability to do something once someone else validates it. Like if someone tells us we're good at something, it becomes easy to believe it. That's because belief is addictive. Many of us don't realise that we have so much proof of how awesome we are at what we do, we just don't see it.

When people compliment us or we receive great feedback from others, that's all positive reinforcement of your strengths and can give you belief and certainty in yourself, if you let it. So if you're looking to increase your confidence, pay attention to the feedback others are giving you, receive the compliments and borrow their belief in you!

**Create A Habit**
Let's talk about certainty. If we know that confidence comes from certainty then the more certain we are, the more confident we'll be. And what's the easiest way to have certainty… Practice.

Often the reason most of us get nervous when we're doing something outside of our comfort zone is because we've never done it before. But when you look back at something that felt really scary before, it doesn't seem as scary after you've done it. Because we have certainty once we've done it. So the key is to build your certainty around going out of your comfort zone and practise it. Consciously make an effort to take steps out of your comfort zone.

The first time it might be terrifying, like in my first live interview with BBC radio, but each time you take the step, it will get easier. Imagine it's like stretching a muscle of confidence. Each time you take a small step out of your comfort zone, you're stretching that muscle to become stronger for the next time.

So what can you do today to push yourself a little outside of your comfort zone? Do something each day that makes you feel a little uncomfortable and each step will build on your confidence.

**Displaying Confidence**
I've shared a lot about confidence coming from within and how to develop more self-belief, but how do you actually show people that you're confident?

For most female entrepreneurs, there is a need to display confidence when talking to new clients, doing Facebook lives or speaking on stages so that others will be confident in working with us.

Whilst it is true that if you believe in yourself then you're more likely to come across as more confident, it's not always easy if you don't know what 'confident' actually looks like.

So here are a few tips that I wish I'd known about being confident when I was building my visibility:

1. **Body Language**

Did you know 55% of all communication comes from our body language? That means that when you're talking to someone, the majority of what they're receiving is based on your body language, not what you're saying or how you're saying it. Therefore, when focusing on building confidence, your strength is in *stillness*.

If you're pacing up and down or fidgeting around, there's an uncertain energy which displays a lack of confidence. Whereas when you focus on being still, whether you're standing or sitting, it will display a strong belief and certainty and therefore, strong confidence.

2. **Tone Of Voice**

Most of the time, when saying something with a doubt in our mind, it often sounds like a question rather than a statement. For example, "We should go on a date" instead of "We should go on a date?"

As you read those statements you will have heard a different tone of voice in your head and that's the same if you were to say them out loud. As soon as a statement sounds like a question, there is an element of uncertainty and therefore a lack of confidence. Instead, make your statements with a certain and confident tone of voice.

3.  **Mind Your Word**

What we say has a huge impact on our self-confidence and the confidence that others see in us. When we are stuttering or using words that show doubt, it gives others the opportunity to doubt us too. One of the most common phrases that does this is "I think".

A lot of people use the words "I think" to share their opinion but when communicating, there's a big difference to thinking and knowing.

So remove the words "I think" from your vocabulary. You may want to use "I feel" if it's a sensitive subject or you want a softer message provided it's delivered with a confident tone of voice.

Someone once told me that if you say anything with enough confidence and certainty, people will listen to you. And from the last six years of building my brand and my business, I couldn't agree more.

Remember, confidence is about how you show up and how you feel about yourself in that moment. So show up in every moment like you're meant to be there.

Stand in your power. Believe in yourself. You've got this lovely.

## About Me

If there is only one thing you need to know about me, it is this – I believe that all women have what it takes to be successful female entrepreneurs and that women have the right to create their own businesses, their own income streams and their own happiness.

I'm a three-time number one best-selling author, an international speaker, multi-award winning entrepreneur and Co-Founder of Queens In Business.

As a chartered accountant at the age of twenty-one and director by the age of twenty-four, my life came to a sharp halt when I was diagnosed with severe clinical depression at the age of twenty-five. After months of growth and recovery, I knew I was meant for more than just the normal path and began my journey of entrepreneurship… little did I know how much of a journey it would really be!

Since then, I've been featured on the cover of Global Woman Magazine, spoken on stage alongside Kim Kiyosaki and have been featured on BBC, Fox, ABC, NBC, CW, London Business Magazine, Business Woman Today, Foundr and more.

Today, I run multiple six figure businesses, including a book publishing business that helps entrepreneurs to become best-selling authors and a global training organisation that teaches entrepreneurs how to grow their visibility and build their authority in the media.

With all of my businesses, my passion and purpose is the same; to help people to reach their full potential using what they already have, whether it's scaling their business, growing their brand or monetising their story.

# Honestly Own It!

### Tanya Grant
Brand Specialist, Founder & CCI
The TNG Designs Group Limited

"The bad news is time flies. The good news is you're the pilot" – Michael Altshuler

You'll thank yourself for it later. Honestly owning what's not working for you, I mean. You've heard of the saying, "it takes a village to raise a child", right?

Well, I believe that it doesn't stop at childhood. I think that support continues throughout life well into adulthood. In fact, even as an entrepreneur, I believe that "village" which will support you in GROWING AND WINNING throughout your life's journey, is paramount.

It's what will help you determine how you fare in the long run, and all those who you love and respect in it will call you out, when and where necessary. Ultimately, it's what will be the basis for how your confidence will grow too.

Have a quick glance at this diagram…

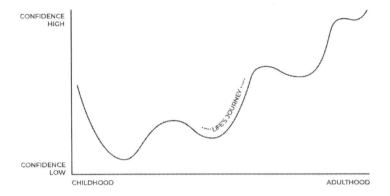

It showcases that throughout life, we'll experience certain downfalls, also known as dips, which tend to shoot down our confidence. They come in the guise of societal bullies who told you "no", discriminations, injustices, bad or even toxic relationships, debt, and/or investments that haven't paid off.

Really, it's the result of anything that's caused you self-doubt in your ability to be successfully you. You'll also see in the diagram, that although those dips continue to happen, over time, they'll eventually get shallower. Why?

Well as we continue to progress, we become more knowledgeable and that knowledge of how to right the wrongs we've experienced, asking for help and actually receiving, listening and learning, are what become our greatest tools. It'll be what will help us to get out of those dips and it'll be what will help to restore as well as strengthen our confidence.

Now don't get me wrong… I'm in no way, shape or form trying to imply that coming out of those dips will be an easy and straightforward process as saying "one, two, three hey presto there you go!" It most definitely is so much more than that. The building yourself back up process is exactly that… a process. It won't happen overnight, there's no such thing as a quick fix when it comes to this.

What *can* be quick however, is that trigger, or "aha", flick-of-the-switch moment I wrote about in Queens In Business' second book, Determined To Rise, that prompts you to action what to do, to get you back on the up.

My one tip straight off the bat for you is to not get caught up in waiting for these moments to happen. They're unpredictable and will be at different times for you and everyone else going through their day-to-day lives. You can't schedule them in… they are what they are and will happen when they're supposed to.

And for an added note, know that they'll be coming from more than one source too. The dips, I mean. They'll even be coming from the ones you least expect. It's what happened to me.

But here's the thing, as much as I don't believe there's a cookie cutter strategy to help you to tackle what happens to you during the 'dips', I do believe that the basis for any kind of impactful confidence-building activity, will always stem from having these three things under your belt…

1. Acceptance
2. Trust
3. Faith

Each of these carry their own weight and as much as I'm about to share with you what some of those experiences were for me, I'd like you to get involved too.

Here's why... If you know anything about the Queens In Business, we're all about taking action. That means doing something about what frustrates the hell out of you. So if you're reading this book, aside from being a supporter of ours which we truly thank you for, I'm guessing that you also have a frustration around the idea of confidence too?

If that sounds like you then be ready to make some game-changing moves and figure out if you're honestly owning any of the points I just mentioned, or resonate with the rest of what I'm about to share with you.

Right now, here's all that I need you to do as you continue reading... Be open to what you start receiving in your own mind, draw acceptance to it and affirm what positive steps you're going to keep making for yourself.

Ready? I'm assuming it's a yes if you're continuing to read this. Okay, let's go!

**Habits That No Longer Work For You**

This is where the importance of that first point comes into play. Acceptance. You'll need this to not only get out of those dips but to also keep your pride parked to one side as you begin to increase your confidence.

I don't need to tell you that this entrepreneurial journey is vast and has its fair share of confidence knockers. Even when you're on the right path towards reaching your 'until I...' value, goal or target, slip ups can still happen. They're inevitable. They're also what will cause you to lose focus, feel lost, feel like you're an imposter and forget all reasoning as to why you're doing what you're doing.

Seems tragic, I know, but they're all very real feelings and emotions. Ask me how I know this…

I remember some time ago when I felt exactly those things. I felt them because I was relying on old habits which, let's face it, weren't very reliable at all and eventually caused me to lose sight of what I needed to pay serious attention to: my finances.

Now I'm mentioning this because it's a sad and all too frequent confidence knocker that happens a lot, especially in the entrepreneurial world. And if it's something that you've been having trouble with… stop ignoring it, accept it and be aware of how it's affecting you. Oh and yes by the way, at times you may be feeling a little incognito, hiding how you're feeling, but those close to you can tell. You see, it's your attitude, your snappier or even confused responses that tell them otherwise and give the game away.

So again, accept what's going on with you, be aware of those feelings and what's going on. Now honestly own that. It's quite freeing.

I remember how during my dip I thought I could handle what I needed to, using old habits like waiting for that "amazing big contract to come through to help me out of all my problems cause that's worked before". Or thinking that it won't be too long till I next get paid from my contract, so I'll handle it all on my own "cause that's worked before". But it wasn't the case at all. Those moments were smaller than I hoped for and sporadic, so weren't enough to cover what I needed. So what did I do?

Well, like the "healthy dose of stubborn" person I am, I kept going with it because I felt like I would be giving up too soon if I tried anything else. Crazy I know, but it's true and in all honesty, I lost sight of my numbers because of it. I was distracted and relied on those old habits working for me again. I should add as well that I wasn't sitting around twiddling my thumbs waiting for those big moments, I kept working on other things to do with my business... The things that I could make sense of because by this point, I'd lost the clarity of my vision.

Things eventually got too much for me and I'd felt it all during that dip. My confidence was especially at an all-time low. You see, what I was once sure of, didn't make sense anymore and where I thought I was putting on a brave face in front of my family, friends and peers, those closest to me, although not knowing what exactly the matter was, could see the stresses weighing heavy on me.

Patience is truly a virtue, but relying solely on that waiting game can send you in a spiral heading in the wrong direction. It was a pivotal moment for me when I started honestly owning and therefore accepting that my old habits weren't working for me anymore.

And here's what also had to happen next.

I stopped ignoring what I was having difficulty with, maintaining and parking my pride firmly to one side because what I used to rely on working for me before was no longer serving me. More importantly, I had to rediscover my resources and ask for help and I felt lighter for doing it too.

Believe me when I say that by making those moves, not only does it start to strengthen you as your confidence slowly but surely builds up again, but it also really humbles you too. I didn't actually realise just how prideful I was until that time in my life.

**I Don't Do Lack!**
For this phrase I'd like to give a BIG thank you to Marie Forleo! I was listening to one of her talks not too long before

writing this chapter and she was explaining the idea of always feeling like she was busy. Over time, Marie started noticing that not only was she showing up "busy", she was also presenting herself and her business as being busy too.

Now you're probably thinking, Tan, where's the harm in that? To you I say, that more often than not, we start to become the words we're saying. Marie realised this and so broke an old habit by replacing it with a new one.

She changed up her language. So she now says to herself, "I don't do busy". By making such a slight adjustment it's given her a huge impact in her day-to-day life and how she now shows up.

This is why now, I don't do lack. That's lack of money, lack of talent, lack of knowledge or know-how, lack of skill, lack of anything… I don't do lack!

In fact, if we ever get the chance to speak face-to-face or when you get to hear me talk at one of our events, you'll hear me come from a place of abundance which reinforces what my brand message is about… helping others to see that they are more than what they see.

And remember when I was referring to the impactful confidence building activities earlier? Constantly doing something like this and not coming from a place of lack, is what will help you to get back to believing in yourself again. You'll start showing up differently with certainty.

Here's why… When I spoke about trust in point number two, it's literally doing what it says on the tin! Trust. Trust in the words that you're saying because they're true. In my case, in spite of what had previously happened for me to make this change and realisation, it's true, I had to trust that I didn't come from a place of lack, only abundance. What I mean by the word abundance is not about throwing caution to the wind and living a hippy, happy, frivolous or carefree lifestyle… It's about thinking and behaving with the idea of openness.

It's another word that carries a hell of a lot of weight and that's why it's one of my core values.

**You Gotta Have Faith**
And now this is where the final point number three, faith, comes into play. To ensure that you build and steadily progress upwards with your confidence, you must believe in, and affirm your faith in, what it is that you're doing and trusting in.

When I'm trusting in what is true to me, I keep on repeating that habit, not only just saying it but believing in it too. The important thing to remember here is that as much as I'm sharing with others, it's all for me and my own growth.

When I say phrases like the one I just shared, "I don't do lack", I'm affirming it to myself. Not to you or anyone else who's around me, just myself, because it's about me. And when you think about it, this follows along the same principles of how affirmations or manifestations work. Because remember, you eventually start to become those words you speak of.

So now, let's bring it back to you. After reading what I shared, what are you not honestly owning, choosing to ignore and wanting to change an old habit for? Remember, be open to what you start receiving in your own mind, draw acceptance to it and affirm what positive steps you're going to keep making for yourself.

As much as your village is there to support you, you're the only one who can make the first move to rebuilding your confidence.

Make that move lovey, you deserve it!

## About Me

Ask yourself... What's the one thing that I'm doing wrong... That I KNOW I'm doing wrong... That I could fix... That I WOULD fix?

I heard this not too long before I wrote my chapter. It was said by Jordan Peterson in an interview with the The Diary Of A CEO podcast creator, Steven Bartlett. They were talking about how to become the person you actually want to be, and it got me thinking particularly about why I chose to go in the direction I did for my chapter. Confidence and the idea of owning the things that might have knocked it down in the first place, is equally knowing the answer to the above question.

It's super key to find out what that is and to address it too as it's what could lead to the reason for why your brand fails or not get the recognition it deserves.

I am a solution-based brand specialist, multi international best-selling co-author, award winning content creator, entrepreneur, public speaker, Founder & CCI of multi-disciplined company, The TNG Designs Group Limited and Co-Founder of Queens In Business. I have collaborated with global brands such as Topshop, Topman, Dorothy Perkins, Burton as well as with Miss Selfridge, and have also helped SMEs in the coaching, beauty, wedding and equine industries too.

At the time of this book being published, I would have had well over 19 years of experience, working in the design industry under my belt and it's fair to say that especially in the branding space, the idea of confidence plays a huge role in a brand's performance. With it, a brand can push its limits, think with abundance or openness so that it can get to the heights of global status – no matter its size. But, without it, a brand can fall by the wayside and be drowned out by the noise of what its competitors are getting up to.

This is why I'm dedicating this chapter to all business owners and entrepreneurs alike who are struggling with re-discovering their confidence. Draw inspiration from this and the other stories you read in this book. Honestly own what's not working for you and know that you are more than what you see.

# Stand Up And Claim What's Yours!

## Carrie Griffiths
Voice Coach for Singers and Speakers
Carrie Griffiths Voice Training

"Every bad situation is a blues song waiting to happen" – Amy Winehouse

My name's Carrie and I'm a "pleaseaholic".

What I mean is, I used to spend my life pleasing people and worrying about what they thought of me. If that wasn't a word before, it is now. I've just decided that it is.

But I wasn't always so upfront. Despite making the decision to become a singer when my daughter was six months old, in the face of criticism (you can read this story in Queens In Business' first book, Time To Reign), being called a "bad mum" and being judged for choosing an alternative life (one that millions of men choose without anyone batting an eyelid), I was actually someone who kept my mouth shut, to keep others happy.

I grew up with very supportive parents and extended family. All of the older generation are very loving and proud of all of us. But every family has its dark moments and, growing up as the child of an abuse survivor, I learned from a young age not to complain. Speaking up for myself meant that I was rude, showing any disappointment meant that I was ungrateful, and asking for anything meant that I was greedy.

Although I knew I was loved, being unable to express my feelings meant that I didn't have a chance to explore and understand them. I was painfully insecure and desperately wanted to be liked. Any emotion besides joy was suppressed until eventually the only "negative" emotions I knew how to express were resentment and anger. But as a woman, especially a Black woman, expressing these emotions are almost always frowned upon.

As a shy extrovert I've always loved being around people. At the age of eight, finding my place as a singer and performer gave me a voice that I couldn't use in my day-to-day life. I danced out my frustrations and sang through my pain and anger. And of course I always used music to celebrate love, laughter and good times.

Being on stage meant that I was able to be in a room or field full of people and interact with them without uttering a word. The more I took to the stage, the more I was able to express my feelings through my performances. My confidence grew as my reputation and audiences grew.

When I transitioned from dancer to singer and decided to take my singing seriously I knew that I wouldn't be able to hide behind my performances forever. I forced myself to talk through my shyness but I had already formed my identity. I had placed my self-worth in the hands of others for so long that when I was on tour performing to audiences of 20,000, I felt that was the only place I felt truly comfortable.

Music even saved me from an extremely abusive relationship where, at one point, I was in fear for my life (you can read about this in our second book, Determined To Rise). But after spending the best part of thirty-three years on stages, I felt empty.

Through the bravado of touring the world, performing to audiences of thousands and selling top ten albums, being a musician means constant scrutiny from managers, promoters, agents, photographers, rivals and even fans. Is she f*ckable enough? Is she agreeable enough? Is she feisty enough? Is she mouldable enough? Is she smart enough? Is she dumb enough? Is she successful enough? Is she English enough? Is she exotic enough? Is she old enough? Is she young enough?

Is she enough? Am I enough?

That was the dark side of my life for years. I always loved performing, but every silver lining has a cloud. Have you ever questioned yourself about something so much you felt like you were losing your mind?

The reality of a touring musician isn't first class flights, champagne and glamorous parties. It's being the only woman in a van full of men sharing dirty pics, talking about last night's porn. It's driving against thick snow in the dead of night, with inadequate heating, so cold that you're huddling under shared sleeping bags to keep warm. It's breaking down in the pelting rain in the middle of the night, waiting on the side of the autobahn for roadside recovery. It's stripping down to as little as you possibly can without ending up in your underwear, pouring water over yourself in a pointless effort to cool down as you chug along at what feels like boiling point to perform, dehydrated, to a sun-drenched crowd.

Okay, these are the extremes. But after years on the road, missing my daughter, birthdays and family gatherings, making the people I met on the way my new friends and surrogate family, something had to give.

I'd been told I was fat and irrelevant one too many times. Then one day I looked in the mirror and said, "F*ck this sh*t!"

I gave up performing as suddenly as I'd decided to give up my marriage and make it my life. It had been my identity for so long that giving it up was more scary than putting up with the gaslighting for a day longer.

At first I felt empowered, I'd given up the very thing that had originally given me the confidence to go out into the world. Or so I thought.

To quote Dave Grohl (again!), "It's times like these you learn to live again". It's easy to feel confident when things are going well. But true confidence is when you're at the bottom of the heap and dragging yourself up to somewhere near any semblance of your former self.

I knew I was good at what I did and threw myself into my job as a music lecturer. I'd taught singing at different organisations for fourteen years so I decided to set myself up as a private voice coach. I put one advert out for £6 and made it back five-fold in one booking. I was self-employed! I loved helping shy singers build confidence in their own abilities not only as a singer, but in countless other areas in their lives.

After three months I was fully booked but couldn't work out how to grow my self-employment into a business. I decided to find a mentor who could guide me in the right direction. With no experience or knowledge of what was out there I chose one of the first I came across.

During one of my first sessions he told me in no uncertain terms, "You can't sell confidence." Looking back I now know that he was simply trying to challenge me to come up with something that sounded a bit sexier. But with that one comment my confidence was knocked clean out of me.

Isn't it ironic?

Up until that point, almost my entire client base was built on helping singers build more confidence. That's the one thing they all said they needed. Every single one. But my mentor had been in business many years longer than me, so he must have been right. Right?

No one person is entirely right all of the time. And, no matter how many mistakes you make, you ultimately know when you're doing the right thing.

**Regaining Self-Belief**

The abusive personal and professional relationships I'd chosen for myself over more than 20 years had led to me stop trusting myself and, ultimately, not having the confidence in my own convictions. I'd gone through multiple physically abusive relationships and survived two bouts of narcissistic abuse. It seemed unfair that the gaslighting and emotional and physical abuse I'd experienced had come to a head and had me second guessing the one thing I had left, with someone I'd gone to for help.

After 14 years helping ordinary people become great singers and 38 years on stage it felt like I had nothing left to offer the world. But I was wrong. And so was he.

It took two years to realise that this one sentence is what had held me back in business for so long. After two years in limbo and a year in "recovery", I have finally forgiven myself for my abusive relationships and other shortcomings. I know that I can help the very people I want to help and achieve anything I set out to do.

Despite the constant voice in my head telling me "You're sh*t at business. Who are you trying to kid? What do you know? You should give up!", co-founding and building Queens In

Business alongside my own business has helped me regain my confidence as a bona fide entrepreneur, business coach and mentor.

I've been selling confidence since the age of eight when I sang my first solo to a full school hall. The buzz I got then is the same buzz I get now when I perform.

When I look back to different events in my life I can see that I've been selling my own self-confidence. From moving to Scotland knowing no one except the cousins I lived with and dancing in the middle of the school playground, to going to boarding school and putting on shows for my housemates, to going to punk gigs by myself because I didn't have anyone to go with, to leaving my husband when my daughter was six months old to follow my dream of becoming a singer, to taking my entry audition for my music degree five times before I was accepted, to selling three top ten albums. My resilience has given me the courage to do the things I believe in and the things that make me happy.

Now things have come full circle and I'm preparing to get back on stage with my new band. As a speaker and singer, fully grown in my own skin, I have created a life in which I can do the things I'm best at: entertaining and serving.

Like a broken bone, when you heal, you'll come back stronger. Courage is not what we show externally. It's the ability to keep going when you feel like giving up.

I used to worry about being vulnerable and telling my story. I'm the woman who left her family to become a singer. I'm the woman who had her head split open by her partner, took him to court and still went back to him.

I used to think that confidence was a result of what we do. But now I know that it's a cycle: when we do something before we feel confident enough, it gives us the confidence to do it again. Then when we've mastered that, we've built the courage to move on to the next step or something new.

Even if your "inadequacies" have been given to you by an overbearing parent, a school bully or a self-obsessed partner, ultimately you are your own harshest judge.

Courage comes with continuously facing your fears. Whatever you're feeling nervous about, give it a go. You never know – it might just work out.

## About Me

I am the Founder of Carrie Griffiths Voice Training, and a London-based singer, international speaker and multi-award winning voice coach, specialising in commercial singing, and conversational and public speaking.

Having been a successful singer for more than twenty years, I have performed in over thirty countries to audiences of thousands, and sold three top ten albums, including a number one.

Drawing from my own experience I help singers and speakers go from hobbyists to professionals, monetise their talents and build successful careers.

At the time of writing I am preparing to release new music with a new band and return to performing after a five year break.

I dedicate this chapter to my band of sisters, my Co-Founders at Queens In Business. They surprise and inspire me every day with their commitment and courage to keep pushing with our vision.

# Never Too Late To Become Unstoppable!

### Julie Fitzpatrick
Rapid Transformational Therapist (RTT), Hypnotherapist and Master NLP Coach
Millieside Therapy & Coaching

"If your actions create a legacy that inspires others to dream more, learn more, do more and become more, then, you are an excellent leader" – Dolly Parton

Have you ever had a time in your life when you wanted to do something but didn't have the confidence in yourself to move forward?

Perhaps you are fearful, and this is holding you back from doing what you want to do?

Maybe imposter syndrome, overwhelm, lack of confidence and self-belief is keeping you stuck from starting up your own business – even though you know you have the skills and experience, but you are not sure where to start. Imagine instead:

- That you have overcome your fear and you know how to take that first step
- You are starting to believe in yourself and have the courage and confidence to move forward

- You know where to learn the skills and have identified the gaps in your life and now you're running a successful business.
- You're living your life with purpose and passion, and you're truly unstoppable!

This is where I am now. But it hasn't always been this way…

**Humble Beginnings**

I was born in 1968 in Essex, England, the second daughter to Freda and Eric. My sister Jackie was two years older than me, and Jane was born three years later. We had a loving childhood and family life. Sure, we had sibling squabbles and fights but nothing major. We all attended the local primary and then comprehensive school. All in all, a 'normal' family. Money was tight, but we had plenty of love and our parents gave us what they could and still do.

During this time, I created a belief that I was just average, and this continued throughout my whole school life and then into adulthood. I believed that if I kept myself below the radar, I would give the impression that I was doing well and that I'm steady and reliable – and then, I would blend into the background.

My fear was that if I was successful, I would be visible and I would draw attention to myself. Once I was in the spotlight people would see through me as the phoney I am, and I would get 'found out'. I didn't want to stand on a pedestal and tell everyone how great I was and what I had achieved because that would be seen as 'showing off' and then there would be comments like "who does she think she is?"

I believed that once I became visible, I would be pushed off my pedestal and that would be humiliating. So why put yourself through that? Stay off the radar, do a good enough job and plod through life.

Education didn't come easy to me and I did have to work hard to keep up. I had friends at school who were high achievers and learning seemed to come naturally to them. I felt I lacked imagination, creativity and I absolutely hated maths. My favourite subject was childcare. I wasn't really one for asking for help either, I would keep my head down and do 'the best I could' and that would be good enough.

I was never in trouble at school, in fact much to the amusement of my husband, I never had a detention, never had a day off sick, never 'bunked off' school and I was a prefect! I always did my homework on time, and I did as much as I could. I was steady and reliable. Wow, that makes me sound really dull and boring.

This way of being and thinking is how (until now) I believed I should live my life. As an adult, I am now looking back and wondering what I could have achieved if I had identified and eradicated this limiting belief years ago. Would I have gone to university and ended up with a completely different life? Would I have been more creative and believed I could do anything I wanted to do? Perhaps I would have been a successful entrepreneur, actress, author, artist, who knows. All I can do now is wonder, but I can't change the past because my past has made me the person I am today.

**Life Changing Decisions**
It's funny, when I was at school I never wanted to work in an office, in fact the complete opposite is true. I wanted to be a nursery nurse. At the time, I needed to do a two year college course, but I only made the shortlist after having done exams and interviews to get a place. I wasn't quite 'good enough' to make the final cut. This was the first insight to the fact that I was nurturing my role as a carer!

So, at the age of sixteen, straight after my exams, my mum took me on the train to London to look for a job. This was in 1985, back then you could walk in and out of a job easily. I remember the day vividly, we walked into a recruitment office called Select Agency in St Mary Axe. The lady there said that she had a job at a company called Gartmore which was literally across the road. She called them up and then said I could pop over the road now for the interview. So off I went, not a clue about the job or how to approach an interview but whatever I did seemed to work a treat and I was offered the job, starting the following week.

A couple of weeks later, I had a call from the college to say they now had a place for me, but I declined as I now had a job in the big smoke earning money. And that is where my life in the corporate world started…

So, in 1985 at sixteen, I am working in London, and have met my first husband Kevin who was seventeen at the time. We were inseparable, and I thought he was the love of my life. In 1990, we both decided we wanted to travel so we quit our jobs and spent a year travelling around Australia and then America. We had a blast, building our confidence as young adults, making new friends, exploring, gaining new life experiences, and creating great memories. Thinking back on this now, that was quite a risky thing to do at twenty-one years of age – moving to the other side of the world, leaving behind family and friends and our secure jobs. We didn't know anyone who had done this before, so I wasn't as average as I thought, plus I was pushing myself outside of my comfort zone.

By 1992, after over a year of adventure we were back in the UK, and I found myself another office job in London. I had realised at this point that this is where the money is. We then bought our first house and in 1994 we got married. Five years later, our son Josh was born. This was now the best moment in my life. However, as any parent knows, our lives would never be the same again…

We made the decision that Kevin would quit his job and be a stay-at-home dad and look after Josh as I earnt the most money. This was both a blessing and a curse.

Remember, this was back in 1999 and a stay-at-home dad was not common. Kevin became very isolated as he was excluded from all the birthday parties, coffee mornings and chats as that was only open to women. Meanwhile, I was struggling because after three months of maternity leave, I was back up in London working twelve-hour days and missing my son like crazy. I felt guilty that I couldn't be at home with him. I didn't really understand his daily routine, I had to ask when to feed him and how much milk he had. As a mother I felt useless and started to resent the fact I had no choice as to whether I could be a stay-at-home mum or even work part-time because I had the pressure to be the breadwinner.

A few years went by and I continued to plod along in the corporate world, being very steady and reliable, getting things done without a fanfare or shouting my success and results to everyone. I didn't particularly put myself forward for promotions, but I ended up progressing up the ladder through hard work and willingness to learn. I did find however, that I wasn't earning as much money as some of my peers and after having another excellent appraisal, I asked about increasing my pay. I was told that the reason I didn't get the same increase was because I wasn't visible enough. I needed to stand out and be seen and learn how to start telling people how amazing I am and what I had achieved. Apparently being excellent at your job, delivering your projects well, on time, on budget and building a great team around you still wasn't enough, because senior management didn't know who I was.

It's only while writing this chapter now, that I have really joined up the dots and realised how the limiting belief that I created when I was young is still at this point holding me back. This fear of being seen and putting myself out there even in my thirties was still suppressing me from becoming more successful. I settled for being average, although perhaps by this time in my life I knew I was slightly above average because I was earning good money, had a nice house, and was having lovely holidays which was more than many of my friends and family. Yet I still didn't acknowledge this and share it with the world.

Over time, my relationship with my husband became more and more strained to the point that we could no longer live together as a family. This took my guilt to another level when we told Josh who was about six at this time that mummy and daddy would no longer be living together as a family. By the end of our relationship, we had been together for nineteen years.

**All Time Low**
It is now 2008, I'm a thirty-nine-years old, single working mum with a nine year old son. Kevin has moved out and we are equally parenting Josh, and with the help of both sets of grandparents we are just about coping with life. Our main priority was always putting Josh's happiness first and foremost.

However, now was my time to get back in the dating world and find happiness for myself. As a parent we devote all our love and attention to our children at the detriment of ourselves. I have since learnt that this is not the best approach for us or for our families. If we are not happy and content with our lives, then this will have a knock-on effect on our family and friends too.

Then I met Andy on a dating app, who I'm happily married to now. On our first date it was love at first sight. At the time of meeting, Andy was a youth worker and as we sat over the dinner table sharing stories about our day, I soon realised that I was bored with my career, and I wanted a job with purpose and passion, just like he had.

Be careful what you wish for because a few weeks later I was offered redundancy from my job of fourteen years. Without hesitation I volunteered for redundancy and by October I was an unemployed single mum in a brand new relationship and turning forty.

Again, as I reflect, this was another huge risk I had just taken. It felt right at the time, but little did I know that a few weeks later there would be one of the biggest stock market crashes ever and suddenly the job market in the city fell through the floor. But that was okay, because I now wanted a 'do gooding job' like Andy. Little did I realise that I wasn't qualified for that kind of work and no one wanted me because I didn't have the relevant experience. I also learnt that they didn't pay very well either and now I had a large mortgage to cover.

I felt like my life had turned into a roller coaster. On the one hand, I had met a wonderful supportive partner but overnight I had gone from a successful working woman to a stay-at-home mum who was unable to get a job. This really knocked my confidence and I felt devastated and wondered if I had done the right thing. I was 'comfortable' in my previous job, not happy but it was all I knew.

Over the coming weeks I spiralled into what I can only describe as a mini breakdown. I was depressed, anxious and always crying. I felt I'd lost my identity and I didn't know who I was anymore. I was used to routine and connection but now, I got up in the morning, took Josh to school and then felt lost. I also felt guilty because I wanted to be at home with him more, but the reality left me empty inside. I didn't know any of the mums at school so I felt isolated. I was used to being around friends at work and we would have a laugh which got you through the day. Now I was on my own, lost and as each day passed, I lost more confidence and self-belief to a point where I didn't think I would ever work again.

During this period, I didn't go to the doctors, I did what was my go-to and 'I just got on with it'. Here I was, a forty-year old woman whose new partner of a couple of months would come round and I would be a quivering wreck, nothing like the confident woman he met only a few months before.

At an all time low, I started to question why Andy would even want to be with me. I then went into self-sabotage mode and tried to push him away because I didn't feel like I was good enough for him. Let's face it, I had no job, I didn't feel fun and didn't feel like a very nice person to be around. Surely, he was having regrets for being with me now? What could he possibly see in me?

Have you ever had a time in your life when you think your life is a mess and you are struggling to know which way to turn?

I knew I needed to find a way out of this depression that hung over me. Luckily for me, Andy did love and believe in me, so I was able to borrow his belief and start getting my life back on track. He was my rock then and he still is now.

I started volunteering at a hospice working in the fund-raising team which I really enjoyed. I felt that I had started to rebuild my confidence and self-esteem. It felt great to be back around people again and share my knowledge and experience. A full-time role came up and I was told to apply but unfortunately the salary was way too low to even cover my mortgage. It was at this point that I accepted that I would have to go back to the corporate world because, financially, this was my only option.

I didn't want to totally give up on finding a new career with purpose and passion in the future so enrolled in a local college to start a four year counselling course.

**Back To The Corporate World**

The thought of having to go back to the corporate world didn't really excite me. I knew that I was gaining confidence, new skills, and knowledge with my counselling training, so that kept me going.

By this time, my relationship with Andy was moving forward and he moved in. His son Luke was now a huge part of our lives. Josh was also settled and happy, I was still volunteering, at college and job hunting. The job market was still poor and finding a role was proving difficult. Again, I felt my confidence diminishing every time I didn't get a response or didn't get a job after an interview. My self-doubt voice got louder and louder as I told myself I wasn't good enough.

Eventually after many setbacks, all my hard work paid off and I was invited to interview for a contract role. I will always be grateful to Ian Bell because he and I worked together previously, and he knew what I was capable of. So much so, he gave me the job without even interviewing me. This was one of the best days of my life because not only had I been offered a job and the money was fantastic but most importantly, Ian had believed in me, and my confidence grew.

A few weeks later, I started the new job, but then the impostor syndrome reared its head. Every time the contract was up for renewal, I expected to be asked to leave. I ended up contracting for nearly ten years. I now know that my limiting beliefs were holding back.

I eventually qualified as a counsellor and volunteered one night a week for many years. I also became a trustee and later Chair of Relate South Essex. At least I was getting my 'do gooding' fix while still earning good money.

Perhaps at this point I should have realised that I'm more than average and I've achieved a great deal in my life. We moved into a beautiful new home, got our puppy Luther (our gorgeous Great Dane) and were enjoying fabulous holidays while I helped transform people's lives.

In April 2016, my contract ended and I decided to take a break to plan our wedding. In July 2016, I married the love of my life on a Caribbean cruise with both our sons and six close friends present. The wedding day was like something out of a fairy-tale and the whole three-week trip was amazing.

**Here We Go Again…**
Back to job hunting. Job market shocking due to Brexit. Limited vacancies. History repeating itself. I could feel myself losing my confidence just like before…

At least this time I had a great CV and track record but even so, it still took me months to find something, but eventually I secured a permanent role.

By the time I was fifty, I was in another corporate role that I didn't really enjoy. I had to stop volunteering because I couldn't cope with it anymore. I was feeling overwhelmed, unhappy, and I'd lost my confidence and belief in myself. I realised I was not living my life. I was going through the motions and was just existing and not particularly coping well. I was always tired, suffering from anxiety, angry, and my emotions were like a rollercoaster. I was struggling to cope with the simplest of tasks at home and at work, tasks that I could previously do easily. Even stringing a sentence together or remembering anyone's names had now become a daily challenge. I thought I was going mad! I had brain fog, and memory loss. The family dynamic kept changing and dealing with blended families and empty nest syndrome all added to the mix.

I later found out these challenges I was facing are symptoms of the perimenopause.

At fifty-two, I was thrown a curve ball in the middle of the pandemic when I was yet again without a job. Part of me was angry and frustrated, but the other part was happy and excited, because I was taken out of a situation that was no longer healthy for me and I needed to make changes in my life. Although this was a bad moment in my life, it was also the best thing that could have happened to me at the time, and the making of me.

**Surround Yourself With The Right People**
September 2020 and it's decision time again. Do I go back to the corporate world or do something different? Luckily for me my close friend Jen Roblin (who I met in the corporate

world and is now a successful anxiety coach) suggested I should follow my dreams and set up my own therapy and coaching business like she did. My initial reaction was, "Don't be silly, what do I know about setting up a business?"

Not much, but that's when I realised that I don't have to do this on my own. It's about surrounding yourself with the right kind of support and Jen initially mentored me to help me get started. Once again, I was able to borrow Jen's belief in me.

I immediately enrolled in neuro-linguistic programming (NLP) training and signed up with Big Business Events who support entrepreneurs to structure and build businesses. I then joined Queens In Business who support female entrepreneurs to become visible. Once I completed my Master NLP, I found Marisa Peer and her astounding Rapid Transformational Therapy (RTT). During this period, I did go back to the corporate world, but this time I went with a totally different mindset. I was doing this to fund my training and to enable me to build my business with strong foundations so when I took the leap, I would already be established.

It wasn't easy juggling life, full-time work, additional therapy training, business training and learning how to use social media. I was also building my client base and enjoying transforming lives. I knew this was where my passion was and I wanted more of this. This was my driver to keep learning and pushing through my fears. I can't tell you how many times I had to push through my comfort zone and feel the fear and do it anyway. Once you start doing this you get addicted to trying new things and then you find yourself saying 'yes' to things more than you say 'no'.

Millieside Therapy & Coaching was born. I learnt that to be successful I would need to find a niche target audience. So, I decided to go with what I knew best. I'm a woman in the prime of life who has suffered from the perimenopause. Life has sent me many curve balls, and I was looking to find my true purpose and passion, to become unstoppable!

**Unstoppable!**
As I worked on my mindset during my NLP and RTT training I uncovered and eradicated my limiting beliefs about myself. I now know that I am enough, I'm amazing and of course I'm far from average. I've gained a new life full of confidence and self-belief and know that I can achieve anything I set my mind to. Such a shame I didn't know this years ago so I could be living my life with purpose and passion earlier!

I now share my own personal success stories as well as those of my client's after having the experience of working with me. In December 2022, I was invited to speak on stage at Queens In Business' Reign Like A Queen event in Kensington, London and I also won the Best Supporter Award. Furthermore, I was featured in a four-page article in the Queens In Business magazine, about breaking down the stigma surrounding women in the prime of their life.

I currently run regular webinars, Become Unstoppable In The Prime Of Your Life, where I teach women how to become unstoppable. I have multiple social media platforms, am regularly invited onto podcasts and stages and now, I'm sharing my story in this book.

I truly believe I am now unstoppable and living my life with purpose and passion. I couldn't have done this without help and support. Remember, it is never too late to believe in yourself and become unstoppable too!

If I can do this, then so can you – now!

## About Me

I'm Julie Fitzpatrick, award-winning Rapid Transformational Therapist (RTT), hypnotherapist, Master NLP Coach and Founder of Millieside Therapy & Coaching. My passion is supporting women to 'Become Unstoppable' so that they can find their true purpose and passion, without being fearful of making life changes.

I am married to Andy Smith, step mum to Luke (twenty-six years), mum to Josh (twenty-three years) and mum to Luther, our nine year old Great Dane. Luther is our resident therapy dog and loves attending any face-to-face sessions.

In December 2022, at the age of fifty-four, I retired from my corporate career after over 35 years, to focus on Millieside Therapy & Coaching. I went on to win my first award for Best Supporter, spoke on the Queens In Business stage, featured in the Queens In Business magazine, appeared on podcasts, lives and interviews – and now, I am a co-autor.

I want anyone reading this book to understand you can achieve whatever you want at any age. Our past doesn't define who we are, it's what we achieve in our future that counts.

Don't be afraid to ask for help. I would not be where I am today without investing in my self-development and learning what beliefs were holding me back. My only regret is that I never did this sooner. I would not have been able to build my business without the help and support of mentors, coaches, friends, and family.

I would like to dedicate this book to my husband Andy for loving and supporting me in whatever I am doing and keeping the family home running whilst I'm off on training or events (which is a lot). Also to my dear friend Jennifer Roblin who inspired me to create Millieside and to follow my dreams. To everyone who has supported me in my life and throughout this journey and to Queens In Business for all the opportunities you have created for me and many other women.

# Discrimination Won't Hold Me Back

## Shelina Ratansi
Director and Founder
SRK Accommodation Ltd

"Believe in yourself and all that you are. Know that there is something inside you that is greater than any obstacle" – Christian D Larson

Shortly after my birth in Zaire, central Africa, in 1971, my parents moved to settle in Uganda. As you probably know, Ugandan Asians faced many problems with the then President Idi Amin who forced them to leave the country.

So, in 1975, my family and I moved to the UK as refugees. It was a daunting experience for my parents in a country with a different culture and values but as a four year old, it seemed like an adventure.

Growing up in Hayes, Middlesex, I rarely saw my mum due to her working night shifts at a factory. Despite her hard work, our family struggled financially as my father was unable to work due to a health condition. However, we found happiness in the close relationships we had with each other as siblings, and the love and harmony within our family. I would spend hours with my dad listening to classic Indian songs. These were some of the best times of our lives.

As a teenager, I took on the responsibility of supporting my mother financially after she became unwell to work due to serious health issues. I accomplished this by taking on a job, working after school and during the weekends. I spent over 26 years working in a management role for a global retail company. However, after being made redundant in 2019, I decided that I no longer wanted to be tied to a traditional nine-to-five job. I wanted to be my own boss.

That's when I started my own business, SRK Accommodation Ltd.

We are committed to providing guests with stylish and comfortable short and long-term rentals in Peterborough, UK. Our mission is to create a home away from home.

But getting to where I am today as a successful entrepreneur has not been an easy ride.

Starting any business carries risks, and it's always possible that the company may not succeed. I have faced the fear of failure many times, having invested so much time, money and effort in my business. I have faced a lot of competition along the way. I have faced difficulties in finding and retaining customers, managing finances, and building and leading a team.

As a Muslim woman who always wears a headscarf, I also had a tough time overcoming racial and gender prejudice in building my business. It continues to impact my ability to grow my business in many ways. But I am aware of my challenges and I choose to take bold steps to address them. How? Let's take you on a journey…

**Invisible And Unjust Barriers**
A few years ago, I approached several letting agents but most of them were not interested. At first, I just thought it was bad luck. But the more rejection I received, the more I wondered what was really going on. I remember one incident that was particularly shocking to me.

I was out with a friend of mine when we came upon a letting agency that I wanted to go into to set up a viewing. She agreed to wait outside while I went in to speak with the agent. I was disappointed to find him uninterested in what I had to say and he kept looking away, which I found disrespectful. Instead, he told me he would leave his card on the desk and he continued working. Ignoring his rudeness, I took the card and exited.

My friend was surprised to see me come out so quickly. I told her that the agent had been dismissive and I wasn't sure if it was because of my headscarf or skin colour. My friend, who happened to be White, offered to go in and request a viewing, and the same agent spoke with her and agreed to set up a viewing for that afternoon!

When we arrived for the viewing, the agent was surprised to see me there and my friend told him that it was me who was interested in the property, not her. I asked him if it was my skin colour or hijab that had made him disinterested. He didn't respond, and I told him that I didn't want to do business with him and left. The experience was shocking and troubled me but made me even more determined to succeed despite discrimination in society.

It is a sad reality that racism against Muslim women who wear the hijab exists. This type of discrimination can affect anyone, regardless of their religion or race. It can happen to people pursuing any career path, and can be based on personal circumstances such as being a single parent or having a certain appearance.

Many Muslim women choose to wear the hijab, a headscarf, and loose-fitting clothing when they are out in public or with males who are not members of their immediate family. Some women also wear the niqab, a garment that covers a large portion of the face. While this is a personal choice, it can unfortunately lead to discrimination and racism. This can include verbal or physical abuse and discrimination in the workplace or other social settings.

It is important to recognise and challenge these forms of discrimination and to support and defend people's right to practise their religion without fear of persecution or prejudice. It is not fair or accurate to make assumptions about someone's beliefs or experiences based on their appearance or cultural practices.

Sadly, discrimination is deeply rooted in broader society and it can manifest in various areas of life, including the world of business. In particular, I have seen a lot of discrimination fuelled by power imbalances that lead some individuals to discriminate against others based on race or gender. These biases can be unconscious or conscious and may manifest in various ways, such as through hiring practices, access to resources, or opportunities for advancement.

As a store manager, I recall feeling disrespected and belittled by certain customers who requested to speak with the "manager" and were clearly taken aback when they saw me, a woman, instead of the male figure they had expected. One particular incident that stands out in my mind is when a customer came into the office and specifically asked for the manager, but upon seeing me, they dismissively asked to speak with my male colleague instead. This behaviour not only made me feel undervalued in front of my colleagues, but also highlighted the persistent issue of gender bias in the workplace.

Discrimination creates barriers and challenges for those targeted. For me, facing racism and sexism had an emotional impact. It resulted in anger, frustration, fear and shame – including low self-esteem, decreased sense of belonging and increased stress. It is so important for entrepreneurs to recognise these forms of prejudice and work towards creating a more inclusive and just environment for everyone.

**Fighting For Justice**

Eliminating discrimination is an ongoing process that requires the commitment and action of everyone in society. As a business owner, lead by example to make your workplace more inclusive and equitable for all team members.

It starts with educating yourself. Read books and articles, research, and engage in profitable and intelligent discussions with others from different perspectives. Get enlightened. Reflect on your own biases and actions and continue learning while growing to create a more inclusive and supportive environment. And *always* speak out and act fast against any discrimination you see.

This is how I have overcome my challenges as an entrepreneur. I hope that you can leverage them for your business too:

1. **Seek support:** Surround yourself with people who can provide guidance, encouragement, and practical assistance. This might include mentors, advisors, colleagues, or friends and family.
2. **Create a plan**: Clearly define your goals and create a roadmap for achieving them. This will give you a sense of direction and help you stay focused.
3. **Take calculated risks:** Entrepreneurship often involves taking risks, but it's essential to be strategic and calculated in the risks you take. Carefully assess any decision's

potential rewards and risks and be willing to adapt and adjust your course as needed.
4. **Use resources:** Many are available, such as business development centres, networking groups and online communities. Take advantage of these resources to get the support and guidance you need.
5. **Stay positive:** Focus on your progress and look for ways to learn and grow from any setbacks you encounter. Reframe negative thoughts and replace them with positive self-talk.
6. **Practice self-care:** Taking care of your physical and mental health can help you feel more confident and capable.

As well as this, it is important to bring your team on board to create a healthy working environment for all:

1. **Establish clear policies:** Make sure that all employees are aware of the company's policies on discrimination and harassment and ensure that there is a transparent process in place for reporting incidents and addressing them appropriately.
2. **Educate your team:** Provide training on diversity, inclusion, and unconscious bias to all employees. This can create a more inclusive culture and ensure everyone understands the importance of treating their colleagues respectfully and fairly.
3. **Encourage open communication:** Encourage open and honest communication within the organisation and make it clear that all employees are welcome to voice their concerns and ideas.

4. **Foster a culture of respect:** Create a culture that values diversity and promotes respect for all employees, regardless of their background or identity.
5. **Evaluate and monitor progress**: Regularly evaluate and monitor the effectiveness of your efforts to eliminate discrimination and make changes as needed. This can help ensure that the organisation progresses and that all employees feel valued and supported.

If you're facing any discrimination, my heart goes out to you. Please continue to be true to who you are and to who you want to be. You have worked hard and persisted in getting to where you are.

Confidence is a feeling of self-assurance and belief in one's abilities. It can be an important factor in personal and professional life, as it can help you take on new challenges, make the right decisions for you, and network with others.
I built my confidence with the support of my husband and son and the network I built around me. I surrounded myself with good mentors and advisors. I set goals to track my progress. I celebrate my success to boost my confidence. I step out of my comfort zone.

Remember that confidence is something that can be developed and improved upon over time. Be patient with yourself and recognise that everyone has moments of self-doubt. The key is to keep building your confidence and not let setbacks hold you back.

**We Cannot Be Held Back**

My business is a success today because of my tenacity and enthusiasm as a female entrepreneur who always aims for high quality. I believe every woman is powerful and capable of overcoming their fears and achieving success.

Over the years, I am proud to have acquired training in different property strategies, expanded the business from one property to nine rent-to-rent properties, built a strong team and culture, been nominated for Female Entrepreneur of the Year 2022, and many other things – I am not finished yet!

I have achieved all of this despite being a Muslim woman refugee facing bigotry. I strongly believe that you shouldn't let society's lack of appreciation for your worth hold you back. Grow and watch all that prejudice disappear.

I don't mention my accomplishments to boast, but rather to highlight something deeper. We are in the 21st century, and as a practising Muslim woman in a male-dominated industry, I didn't let myself be underestimated. My determination inspired my husband and son to get involved and help grow the business. Our goal was to make all of our properties the top choice for short and long-term rentals in Peterborough, catering to corporate travellers, vacationers, and contractors using Airbnb. We worked towards making our prices competitive and the quality of our offerings the best it could be.

As successful as I have become, I still proactively look for opportunities. You can't stop where you are. There is someone out there doing far better than you are and as an individual that business is the competition you have to outrun. Once you stop growing, you could be on the way down. Strive to stay relevant no matter what.

I am determined to reach a lot of women so that regardless of their religion or the discrimination they face, they can be successful. I want to prove that obstacles can be overcome. As a Muslim woman, I am determined to demonstrate that my challenges do not define or limit my potential for success.

It is important to remember that you have the right to be treated with dignity and respect, and you should not let discrimination hold you back from pursuing your goals. It is never acceptable to experience any form of discrimination, and it is important to stand up for yourself and speak out against discrimination when you see it happening to others.

Being a part of Queens In Business gave me the confidence and opportunity to share my experiences and inspire others to pursue their dreams. I'm excited to share my story and help aspiring female business owners to increase their knowledge and become influential participants in discussions about important issues facing society. Every woman is powerful and has the potential to overcome difficult circumstances and achieve success.

I exist, and so does the book you have in your hands, but every single word I have written will not come to life until you practically put these solid experiences into good use.

## About Me

My name is Shelina Ratansi and I am the Founder of SRK Accommodation Ltd based in Peterborough. We provide fully furnished, stylish, short and long-term accommodation in making your stay feel like a home away from home.

Setting up SRK Accommodation enabled me to put into practise what I was passionate about, and this is reflected in the interior of our properties. I am thankful for the great feedback and reviews that we receive, which gives me more ideas and motivation to continue to build my portfolio and let my creativity flow.

In all my work, I want to inspire others to strive to make the world a more inclusive and accepting place for all. I would like to dedicate my chapter to people who are looking for inspiration and motivation to follow their dreams and pursue their passions.

# Confident Leadership

**Tess Cope**
Coach & Consultant
The Transformation Agency

"Confidence is the stuff that turns thoughts into action" – Richard Petty

23.03.2020 – 10 years in the making and in a heartbeat, it felt like it was falling around my ears.

Can I survive this? Shall I just quit? So many business owners were taking this moment to fold and have an easier life. I knew I could jump on the bandwagon without too much noise. It would seem like a perfectly reasonable response.

These were just some of the provocative questions that were tumbling around in my head. Endlessly.

My clients, a lot of who are global organisations, had been getting increasingly nervous about the potential impact of the pandemic. The distorted stories and guarded updates coming out of Asia PAC were becoming more worrying and then, IT moved into Europe. The veils were taken off and the potential scale of what we were facing was horrific.

As a human race, this was a catastrophe that would challenge every dimension of life. And although we wouldn't wish to experience this ever again, there have definitely been many life lessons that I hope we never forget. For now, I will focus on the lessons that have built my confidence as a business owner and entrepreneur.

Business plans with clients were suddenly under a big fat pause button. Whoever said big organisations can't move fast are mistaken – when they need to, it happens.

I launched my business in 2010 coming out of the last big recession and had built it to mid-six figures, almost single-handedly. Yet there I was with almost zero in the bank and an empty diary. I hadn't invoiced anything for a few months and up until now, that wasn't a concern – there was plenty in the pipeline.

The first few weeks were a bit of a rollercoaster. I had many sleepless nights of constantly berating myself. I had allowed myself to become exposed. I felt vulnerable. I felt frustrated and empty. The truth is, I felt like a failure. Let's just say, my self-confidence was having a bit of a vacation.

In times of trauma, we can get triggered into fight, flight or freeze mode. I was frozen. At least temporarily.

Then life has a way of waking us up.

Our youngest daughter, who had left home a few years before, picked up the courage to share that she was having anxiety attacks, and that the constant news of the pandemic was making it worse. She needed our support. She needed to have a sense of safety.

As any parent would do, we encouraged her to move back home with her little boy. It never ceases to amaze me what we can 'pull out of the bag' when we decide to help others in desperate need, yet when it's exclusively for ourselves, we can be a bit slower off the mark. This was the trigger that shifted me into action.

I took the lead – in the same way that I encourage the leaders I work with to do. I introduced a new routine at home, which would support our mental health and our physical well-being. Every Monday to Friday, 9am, we did the Joe Wicks PE workout. Let's just say, there were a few swear words amid the sweat. But this gave our days some structure and a routine that elicited some energy and positivity. After a few weeks, we even added a plank challenge – which got pretty competitive.

Positive family routines in place, I then decided to offer my support to my clients. They weren't in a position to pay for my coaching or team facilitation services, but that didn't mean they didn't need it. In fact, the opposite was true, so I offered my support, with no expectation and trusted that mutual exchange would prevail in the longer term. This kept me in conversation with the market – I was visible, available and adding real value.

Like most of us, I took the opportunity to consume as much online learning as possible. One of my long held ambitions had been to write a book, but I honestly never thought I would have the time, space or ability to do it. Low and behold, lockdown pushed one of those excuses off the list pretty sharpish.

So I decided to do what I'm good at – have great conversations and really listen for the key themes. I reached out to as many people in my network that fitted my ideal reader profile (which was also my ideal client) and asked them if they would be happy to help with some research. I asked them what they would want in a book about coaching (my chosen field of expertise) and explored what a great book meant to them.

These conversations helped to generate valuable research and boosted my confidence and intentionality for my first book. But they did more than that – they triggered conversations about how I may be able to help in their broader people development agenda when the world opened up again. This initiative alone helped nurture my business back to 50% of what it had been, within 12 months.

A fundamental human need for survival and especially during times of change, is the need to belong. In this locked down universe, I had a strong need to find my tribe of fellow business owners. I wanted to find like minded souls who were fighting their way out of the trenches and back up the mountain. After some research, I signed up to a mastermind. It is one of my best investments and I'm still part of this mastermind group today.

In addition to being part of a great community, I clawed my way back by working on a series of 90 day sprints. Within our group, we each set and shared our targets for the period ahead and we had a group coach cheering us on. This sponsorship sometimes took the form of a much needed sharp dig in the ribs. We cheered and championed each other. We found a place where it was okay to talk about the effort, the small wins and the days where we felt despair. It was phenomenally helpful.

So here I am, a few years on. I have brought the business back to where it was before and beyond. I've built the team and published my book. I've had great feedback about 'HARNESS – a systemic approach: guaranteed to revolutionise your coaching.' I was blown away and humbled to have been voted Inspirational Leader of 2022 at the Queens In Business Awards, and particularly grateful because I know that most of those votes came from clients.

I've recently heard a well-researched definition of confidence that speaks to me: confidence is the stuff that turns thoughts into action. I've captured below, what I have learned about moving from my own freeze mode during the pandemic into consistent action.

**1. Create Healthy Foundations**
Start by prioritising your mental and physical health. These are foundational. It doesn't need to be a dramatic plan – it's more about small consistent steps. We did the Joe Wicks workout for 15 mins each morning but it set the tone for the

rest of the day and created consistency. Consider if you'd find it helpful to partner up with someone to keep you accountable.

2. **Find Your Tribe**

Our most fundamental human need is to belong. Find those kindred spirits – join a business community where you can dig into the detail, where it's okay to talk about the challenges of your business, and where you can also celebrate and own your successes.

Be careful that you don't over-index on fitting in though. Be you – there is only one you and it's easy to get lost. Take some time to invest in your self-awareness – know what matters to you. What do you stand for and what will you stand against? When you are clear on these core values and are consistently aligned to these, you are perceived as more reliable. When you are more consistent in your behaviour, trust and credibility builds within your tribe and just as importantly, with your clients.

3. **Confront Your Reality**

Be honest with yourself about where you are starting from and know that it is okay to ask for help. This help might be in the form of peer-to-peer coaching but it can also be practical help, like the bounce back loans that were made available by the government during the pandemic.

Do some research. Get clear on what is essential at the phase of your business journey. For some sectors, a website is more of a 'nice to have' – it might be more about your social media profile and building your audience. And don't try to be everywhere all at once. It's better to focus on two main platforms and build momentum from there.

**4. Create Hope For The Future**

Hang in there – everyone has been there at the start of this entrepreneurial journey, and sometimes more than once!

Get clear on why you do what you do. This sometimes needs to be reviewed as your core values evolve over time. I've just spent some time reviewing this aspect myself and I'm clear that the purpose of my business is to positively impact 100,000 people's working lives.

Because I'm working with medium and larger organisations, and at the leadership level within those businesses, this is possible for us. Helping to build healthy organisations and positively impacting the working lives of people is what gets me out of bed in the morning. It fills me with energy, purpose and is deeply fulfilling. It matters.

Start with 90-day sprints rather than an annual plan. Identify the actions that it will take to deliver on your plan. Think about the inputs and your desired outcomes. Be realistic with what it will take and what is possible in this period of time. It always amazes me how quickly this time evaporates.

A 90 day plan gives you enough time to experiment, to learn and to adjust. It provides the chance to celebrate the small wins. Decide at the start of each 90 days, what your reward will be.

During the pandemic, I decided to set my target on getting things set up such that we could bring my horses home. It took me a series of four 90 day sprints to generate the capital needed but it was worth it. Before this, my horses were in an expensive livery and it took me up to three hours each day for travel and their care. Having the horses at home for me, was and still is, a game changer that impacts every aspect of family life.

I do hope this chapter has ignited something in you and given you confidence that you too, can start from wherever you are, and find your way up the mountain. I hope these suggested steps help you to move from thinking about things, into action – step by step.

## About Me

After 20 years of working inside organisations at various levels of leadership, I take my place alongside leaders – in my role as coach, facilitator, consultant and cheerleader.

I care about creating healthy systems where the best people want to work and perhaps more importantly, want to stay because we each spend a big chunk of our life at work – whatever that means for each of us. I want to play my part in ensuring that's a good experience.

I set up my business, The Transformation Agency in 2010, just as we were coming out of the last recession and whilst this experience served me well, nothing prepared me for the pandemic of 2020.

My business, which was predominately reliant on a face-to-face model, crashed. I was left with almost nothing despite 10 years of passion, dedication and hard work. It was a moment where I had to call on an inner strength, and fully step into my leadership.

This chapter describes how I pulled myself out of a frozen state and clawed my way back up the mountain. Because leadership is about being courageous enough to go first, authentic enough to be you whilst confidence is the stuff that moves you from thinking about it, to actually doing it.

I dedicate this chapter to those business owners who are facing some challenging times right now – hang in there – it will be worth it.

# Reborn

## Rajni Singh
Nutritionist & Fitness Coach

"Not everything that is faced can be changed, but nothing can be changed until it is faced" – James Baldwin

I remember that night vividly. I was due to embark on a brand new chapter in my life. Sitting down to eat dinner with my beloved family in India before flying to the UK the next morning to start newly married life. I was on an emotional roller-coaster, feelings swaying between anxiety and fear but also excitement about what the future could hold.

My father's eyes were full of worry – his little girl who he had always been so proud of was about to fly the nest and would soon have to stand on her own two feet. I knew he was happy for me and trusted my capability to make him proud no matter where my path led me.

I was born in a small city in India, to two doting parents who proudly raised all five of their children equally regardless of gender. Being the youngest daughter however, I was privileged and showered with affection. The love and support I received from my parents and siblings has been unconditional and selfless. No matter what came my way they were always behind me.

I attended a Catholic school and I was completing my Masters when I got married at the age of twenty-one. Growing up I was quite an introvert. I suffered with anxiety and experienced feelings of self-doubt and fear of judgement but having said that, I have always been ambitious, strong-minded and full of aspirations with a passion for sports and fashion.

Little did I know that I would be expected to find my own strength, to lay strong foundations for my marriage and forge new relationships with no real knowledge of where to begin. Suddenly this young girl had to become a woman with responsibilities. My whole life would profoundly change. I had to put all my dreams and aspirations aside and learn to fit in with a new family, new culture and figure out how to be someone's wife.

**The Adjustment Period**
It was a challenge to adjust to the new culture and community. Especially coming from having a strong support system in my family, it forced me into independence and I had to start all over again. Being an introvert didn't help. I began to feel lonely, missing the presence of my father who was my pillar of strength, missing my mother's warmth and the friendship of my sisters and younger brother. I learned how to master the art of handling all my responsibilities while keeping a smile on my face, despite how I felt inside.

I always considered myself to be accommodating by nature, but somewhere along the way I became compromising instead. I was constantly trying hard to fit in, to feel a sense of belonging. I sacrificed both my personal and professional life in favour of pleasing others as their opinions mattered a lot to me. I acted the way society had expected me to behave.

At some point, I lost my own voice, knocking my confidence, leaving me feeling unworthy. Like many women, I spent so much time prioritising others that I lost myself. I forgot to have fun and enjoy the little things in life. I resigned myself to a life of no confidence, scared to speak up for myself. I didn't know how to lay healthy boundaries or to say 'no'. I settled into a routine, seeking perfection and became hyper-critical of myself. I became angry over petty things, constantly worrying about chores and to-do lists. I forgot to relax.

Life had become robotic. I sacrificed a social life in favour of maintaining balance in other aspects of my life. This left me feeling bereft, questioning is there more to life? I chose to remain questioning for fear of judgement, especially as women within South Asian cultures are conditioned to be seen and not heard. The more I tried to suppress these feelings, the more they crippled me with anxiety. The constant emptiness had started to engulf my life, leaving me constantly feeling on edge. However, there was a fire inside me that was not prepared to settle for average, I had to find myself again.

**Motherhood**
Motherhood brought its own challenges and I suffered postpartum depression after the birth of both of my children.

I had no idea at the time that that was what I was dealing with but in hindsight, I can clearly see the effect it had on my mental wellbeing. The monotonous routine of juggling parenting and chores left me mentally exhausted, however I never had the courage to admit it. Taking time for myself wracked me with guilt but that little escape to the gym on a weekend revitalised me.

I returned to work after my second child was born as my mother-in-law stepped in to help me with childcare. I helped my husband in the family business for four years, took a part-time role within the NHS, allowing me to focus on self-development and giving me some differentiation between home life and business. During that role, I realised my vulnerability was taken for granted.

I suffered under the wrath of a poor manager who stumped my professional growth. I hadn't yet regained my confidence nor developed the ability to set boundaries at work. I felt unworthy and incapable, preventing me from seeking alternative employment. I felt stuck and even though I longed to quit, I simply knew no way of acting on those feelings.

Through the power of prayer and the faith of God, I gathered the courage to face the consequences. I resigned, and to my surprise, I was offered a new job the next day. I began to value a better working environment and supportive team mates. I began taking baby steps towards improving my confidence, but things were not smooth-sailing, my emotions were not allowing me to move on. Thinking of my past always made my chest heavy with sadness. I couldn't seem to heal my internal wounds. I suffered with panic attacks and withdrew into a solitary world of worry and insecurities.

I noticed certain traits in my own daughter's behaviour at the age of eleven. She had become shy, seeking approval from others and too afraid to express her own opinion. I could clearly see my own reflection of who I had become in her and I hated to see that. I knew I had to change but had no idea how I could break the cycle.

There was a clear correlation between my behaviours and my relationships. My inner voices berated me constantly. The more I dwelled on those thoughts, the more I became anxious and hopeless. I wanted to fix all this but would not say a word to anyone. I had to stay strong for everyone else, as expected of me. I didn't know anything other than to be a good mother, wife and daughter-in-law. I had become an expert in prioritising the needs of others rather than my own. I mindlessly went on daily, stuck in the rut of continuity. My life had become stagnant. Everything was evolving except me!

I underestimated myself, doubted my capability, refused to acknowledge my strengths and focused too much on what I couldn't control. Anxiety crippled my ability to focus. I didn't want to live like this.

In 2015, I faced another setback with my physical health. I was diagnosed with PCOS in adolescence and suffered with severe acne throughout my thirties. A PCOS diagnosis affects you both physiologically and emotionally. I suffered multiple health concerns such as back problems, shoulder impingement, a herniated disc in the neck and lower back, vertigo and tinnitus. Battling chronic pain had become a part of my day-to-day life.

Medical professionals struggled to find the root cause and offer solutions to my concerns for almost two years. During this time I could not drive, exercise or perform normal day-to-day activities. Life had become confined and miserable. Some days I found hope, on others I felt hopeless.

The major battle was between me and my inner demons. I never imagined that stress would affect my mental wellbeing to the extent that I didn't want to continue living. I had hit rock bottom, feeling worthless and losing trust in life. I refused to be a victim, I knew I had to stop expecting someone else to swoop in and fix me, deep down I knew that I held the key to change.

**Transformation**

I came across a fitness community called "Fittr." I lurked in the background for some time, but resonated with the incredible stories shared by the users and I realised I was not alone. Fitness had changed their perspectives and helped them overcome their own challenges.

In May 2021, I participated in an online 12 week transformation challenge, setting myself a goal to follow a structured routine. I had to eat quantified food which required preparation and discipline. The challenge kept my mind off anxious thoughts.

I learnt to prioritise my tasks according to their importance and value. I learnt to control my impulsiveness. It felt good to manage things better with more energy and less stress, it enabled me to rationalise my thoughts easier. With guidance from my fitness coach and my own dedication and consistency, I ended up placing in the top 50 of 42,000 participants.

My fitness journey was a life-changing experience, I truly felt like I was reborn. As I became physically stronger I also became mentally stronger. I was so proud of my achievement; I had earned the accolade myself. I could clearly see the benefits of regular fitness and quantified nutrition. My acne had improved, my periods regulated, no more chronic pain, postural improvement and I learned to practise mindfulness. I began to feel happy again. The challenge liberated me from my negative thoughts, and settled my inner turmoil, restoring my connection to my true self. I was confident and passionate like never before, emerging like a phoenix who had found a greater purpose in life. Finding ways to be her best version, to grow and learn. I had learnt to prioritise my own wellbeing.

Who knew that one day, my escape to the gym would become my passion? I was bursting with energy, my performance at both work and in my personal life improved. I was able to battle my anxiety. I found joy, I felt worthy! I had never felt so confident in my own skin before.

So I decided to turn my passion into a profession. I mastered the tools that had helped me achieve something that I had thought was impossible and used them to empower others to transform, and find their best selves.

Confidence is just like a muscle, the more you work on it the stronger it becomes. The more I faced my fears, the calmer I became. Focus on facing your fears directly, slowly and gradually instead of allowing your inner demons to make you feel incapable of achieving your goals.

**Pushing Boundaries**
In March 2022, I became a qualified nutritionist and fitness coach. Desperate to unlock my full potential, I felt a tingle inside me telling me that now is the time to seize every opportunity. Since a very young age, I had dreamt of walking a runway. I applied to participate in the UK's longest running beauty pageant, Miss Great Britain.

I tentatively shared my idea with my husband and to my surprise, he encouraged me to compete. Competing would mean conquering my biggest fear of public speaking and stepping outside of my comfort zone. Within my culture, it's relatively unheard of to see a forty-one year old married woman with children taking part in a competition like this, especially in swimwear.

I wanted to set a positive example for all women, especially South Asian women, who may have lost themselves like I had. It was my opportunity to prove to others that it is never too late to follow your dreams and grow as a person. I'd never taken part in a pageant so I had no idea what to expect. I found out that I was the only woman ever within my category's history who was born and raised in India.

I attended a masterclass in preparation for the main event. Upon entering the room, at first I felt overwhelmed. My confidence levels dropped, my anxiety peaked and I felt as if I was out of my depth. I managed to rationalise and overcome those negative thoughts with a little motivational self-talk. I understood that I couldn't control the outcome of the competition, but I could be myself and give it my best shot and choose not to worry about being judged. Those 15 minutes of self-talk changed everything.

I focused on getting to know others, sharing stories, making new friends, supporting others and most importantly enjoying the overall experience. I had never seen so many empowering women in one place. I felt inspired!

My experience at Miss Great Britain changed my whole attitude towards myself. The whole journey forced me to do some soul searching which helped me connect with my true beliefs, my inner potential and both my strengths and weaknesses. I had found myself again!

My mentor, Kat Henry, really helped me unlock my potential. She helped me focus on my strengths in preparation for my pageant interview. As I put pen to paper, the more I discovered my true self, growing in confidence and ready to face any challenges head on.

The competition finale was an extraordinary experience, from the opening dance to strutting in swimwear to feeling glam in an evening gown. It felt magical, nothing less than a fairy-tale. My younger self would've been so proud. I felt like daddy's little girl again, fearless and charismatic, but this time it was my husband and children cheering proudly for me from the audience. That moment was priceless. Placing in the top five evoked a feeling that I had not expected. I felt a surge of alien emotions, full of happiness, pride and a great sense of achievement. I truly experienced what I had read in those inspirational books – when you are inspired by a greater purpose the universe conspires to help you achieve that goal by embellishing you with strength and determination.

My tips would be to set small achievable goals and work towards them individually. Be grateful and praise yourself for all achievements, large or small. It's a continuous process. It is important to consistently practise self-reflection and maintain a positive mindset. Confidence is a skill that can be learnt over time but it starts with trusting your intuition. It can be overwhelming but if you start small and stick with it, it is possible. Without fail, I remind myself every morning that I am capable, strong and enough. I have the courage to stand strong to face any challenges life throws at me. Life is all about experiences and lessons.

I never understood before how to be myself unapologetically. I cared far too much about others' opinions. It took me a long time to get to where I stand today and it is an ongoing journey. When I look back at my progress, I am proud to see how my fitness journey helped me physiologically, mentally, spiritually and socially.

Confidence is something that you can work on by taking small steps towards knowing yourself first, establishing your beliefs and celebrating yourself for who you truly are. I truly understood the meaning of life when I turned inwards and tried to listen to my deep inner voices and block the external noises. This has turned me into a woman of resolute character. A woman is not prepared to give in but instead, find opportunities because life is full of possibilities. You just have to change the narrative.

**Growth Is An Ongoing Journey**
By profession, I am a practice manager within the NHS. I am also a certified nutritionist, fitness coach and a social media influencer. My main goal is to raise awareness about fitness, mental health and overall wellbeing. My ethos is to help others transform both physically and mentally too by encouraging them to build consistent and healthy habits.

Helping them to make incremental steps towards building a healthier lifestyle, we focus on understanding the power of combining a balanced diet with regular exercise. I aim to help them find the right tools to build both their physical and mental strength allowing them to become the best versions of themselves. Making a difference in someone else's life is a priceless gift. Helping others gives me a huge sense of achievement – it is such a satisfying feeling encouraging others to push their boundaries and watching them succeed.

From a person who was always scared to try new things, afraid to take on risks, I have grown into someone who is always ready to take on challenges head on, with a positive attitude. I learnt to widen my horizons by laying healthy boundaries, prioritising what is important and practising better time management. I endeavour to be open to challenges and actively explore every possibility around me. I take each day as it comes. Prioritisation allows me to create plans, but divide them into smaller, achievable goals. I had to learn to focus on working on the immediate goal rather than the end result. This allowed me to remain consistent and motivated, thus enabling me to give each plan the full attention it deserves on my timescales.

I am a student for life. I have a strong determination to keep evolving in both my personal and professional life. For that, it is very important to surround yourself with like-minded, positive people because energy bounces back. Be prepared to face set-backs but don't let them defeat you. It is a good idea to associate with mentors. Guidance is imperative for growth and fine-tuning your skills.

If I could offer you some advice… It took me 40 years of my life to gather the courage to believe and embrace myself for who I am and to do something for me. I would like to remind every woman out there who resonates with my story that you cannot continue to pour from an empty cup. It's okay to make yourself a priority. Stop living with the guilt of desiring to follow your dreams. Do anything that you are passionate about, that brings you inner happiness. It does not have to be something big.

Remember, YOU control your thoughts. When you limit your thoughts you limit your growth. Change happens when you are willing to make a small shift in your mindset from "I CAN'T" to "I CAN". Once you take your first courageous step towards your goals, everything starts falling into place. There are no mistakes in life, only lessons. There is no such thing as a negative experience, only opportunities to grow, learn and advance along the road of self-mastery.

What you go through grows you. Even pain can be a wonderful teacher. When one door closes, another one opens if we open our mind to learning in every event. This way we grow to be stronger and happier. When life knocks you down, you have two options: one, be a victim and say "life is not fair" or two, utilise the resources around you and make positive change.

Like many, I find life hard. However, I have discovered the importance of using my voice and asking for help when needed. Today I am living a richer life that money cannot buy. This was all possible by making conscious choices for me and taking full accountability of my actions. I am doing what I love and that drives me and keeps me motivated.

Life is full of possibilities, you just need to change the way you look at things.

## About Me

I am a fourty-one year old wife and working mum, living with my in-laws in a joint family in the UK. By profession, I am a certified nutritionist and fitness coach. I also work as a practice manager in the NHS and recently became the fourth runner-up in the Ms Great Britain beauty pageant 2022.

I come from a culture where women were often not heard or seen. They often gave up on their dreams to fulfil other roles in life. I was one of them. Like many women, I was someone who had lost my true self somewhere in my journey. I stopped believing in myself, lacked confidence, and was afraid to speak up. I was someone who was always seeking validation.

It was only through my fitness journey that I was able to know my true potential, overcame my fears and dared to dream big. By confronting my fears head on, I was able to resurrect my confidence, self-image and self worth. I am now emerging like a phoenix who is confident and passionate like never before, who has become resilient and who is determined to let no one dim her light.

Now, I am determined to encourage women all across the world to build both inner and outer strength, inspire them to push their boundaries and help them form consistent and healthy habits and be the best versions of themselves.

I would like to dedicate this chapter to my husband who didn't stop believing in me even during the times I doubted myself the most. He saw something in me that I could not see, I am grateful that he encourages me to dream big.

# Gem Made Under Pressure

**Olufunmilola Olatunde**
Property Investor
Oruninc Relocation

"I can be changed by what happens to me. But I refuse to be reduced by it" — Maya Angelou

*Trigger warning*

I was born into the family of Mr Ezekiel Olaniyi and Adelaide Ronke Olatunde on a cold winter night on 9th February 1965. The second child of four, and middle child for seventeen years, with an inquisitive mind and curiosity welded to my bone marrow.

Born in the former beacon of the Western Imperialist empire, I soon returned to the home of my parents and ancestors before them, back to Nigeria. Growing up in Nigeria, freshly uncoupled from Britain's colonial rule and still in the process of deciding how the tools of her former master would be integrated with the heritage and culture, this time was crucial in shaping me into the woman I am today.

However, it was not so difficult to wonder how different my life would have been had I remained in the UK, not simply because of the different people I'd have met and the choices they'd elicit, but down to the difference in the staunchness in

---

[1] Suicidal ideation and emotional abuse

the ideology when it came to discussions of age and gender, for in Nigeria, a woman's capabilities were limited and a child was to be seen and not heard.

That isn't to say I didn't have love in my home. I had a loving parent – my dad, but he was unable to show that love in any other tangible way than ensuring that everything I physically needed was provided. As for my mum, while growing up, I never once heard her say 'I love you'. I was never hugged and I never felt comfortable being myself.

We were three sisters for a while, but I was treated differently by my mum. I can't remember any of our interactions being pleasant. I had always thought I'd done something wrong, something to spite her and poison her against me. It wasn't that she was incapable of love, I'd watched her heap it upon my younger sister. No, she was choosing to despise me, and probably for something I had no recollection of doing.

Perhaps the memory had faded for her too, and the vitriol I felt from her was reflexive; a subconscious response to my mere existence. Nonetheless, this malice was channelled, reinforced and made through comparing the three of us against each other, specifically around grades.

Anything less than a first to my mum was not acceptable, but for me it went deeper than that. When I failed to meet these lofty expectations, I was not reprimanded, but belittled. Every year, I was told I was a failure, couldn't make it, I wouldn't amount to anything, or a combination of all of these.

At fifteen, I was finding it difficult to read or see the blackboard. When I confided in my mum, she dismissed me, claiming that I wanted to wear glasses for fashion and that nothing was wrong with me. At that point, with everything I'd endured, I began to question what the point of living was, and eventually decided to take an overdose of paracetamol to end my life and with it, all the trouble that I had been suffering.

However, my plan was foiled when my mum found me and took me to the hospital, where my stomach was pumped. That was the day I realised that God still had a plan for me in mind, and he couldn't let me die then.

Back to school and studying, but there was little change on that front, and my first attempt at GCSE had me coming up short for the required grades. My dad suggested that I return to Year 10 and spend the next two years preparing for the exams. He even went as far as becoming my teacher in the evenings, after working all day as an economist. When I took the GCSEs again, I was able to make the grades and headed off to college. It was there I met my first husband (Michael Olujide Olubode). We didn't go to the same college, but he'd come with a friend to some event happening at my college. We met and became friends before he proposed.

**Alien Land**

My passion is helping people. I want people around me to be better by helping them release their potential so I decided to become a doctor. But unfortunately getting admission would mean sitting more exams. However, I was determined and tried multiple times, but couldn't make the cut-off point to be admitted into university.

Eventually, it dawned on me that, as opposed to rotting in Nigeria, I could return to the UK. So, I brought my intentions to my dad and initially, he objected. However, he later softened and agreed that if I met two conditions I could go: the first was that I gained admission to a university or get a job, and the second was that I bring my boyfriend – who I revealed had asked me to marry him – home to meet them. I agreed to the terms and we began processing my passport, which ended up taking about a year to complete.

I introduced my then boyfriend to my family in December 1988, a nerve-wracking event that thankfully passed without issue, and a year later, on the final day of 1989, I departed from the home I had been raised in and landed in an alien world. I didn't know where to start or what to expect, but my curiosity made me excited to learn and embrace it all, with the safety net that was my aunt and uncle with who I was staying. Unfortunately, that safety net was a façade, because within a week, I was chased out of my supposed safe haven and I had to fend for myself.

First, I had to register with an agency so that I could start to earn money to make a living. I rented a room in a house with a multiple occupancy and managed to get a catering assistant job at the BBC in White City. The chaos of it all left me more than a little homesick, but there was no way I was returning home. Not to prove my mum right when she had belittled me. So, I got a second job at a bingo hall in Shepherds Bush. On top of all that, I was looking to find a way to achieve my dream of working in a hospital.

I started out by applying for any and every trainee post I could find, and even though there was no word from any of them, I kept applying and praying to God that something would come along soon. As faith would have it, something did, and I found out when my referee called to say that he had been asked for a letter of reference from Royal London Hospital and that I had been called in for an interview.

The interview was a success and I got the job as a trainee biomedical scientist. I was over the moon at being able to fulfil my ambition, so much so that I reached out to the uncle and aunt that had driven me out of their house to tell them about the good news. Little did I know that they did not share in my joy. Instead, this only hardened them against me, envious that I was a British citizen by birth. But none the wiser at the time, I excitedly moved forward into my new life.

**Deceit And Devastation**

By the end of 1991, I was thriving. I was loving my job, I had bought my first home – a two-bedroom house in Eaglestone, Milton Keynes, and was looking to the future. Now, what comes next when you have a house and have secured a job? Well, according to my culture, the next thing is marriage! And I already had a man waiting for me back in Nigeria. So, I called my parents and told them to start planning my wedding for the summer of 1993, as I would have finished my exams and would be able to come home for a month. At that time, we would have the wedding and I would sort out my husband's papers and return to the UK.

Little did I know that it would be a loveless marriage. When the time came, everything went as I had outlined and when I left Nigeria at the end of the summer, I returned to the UK to wait for my husband to join me. That time, I lived in ignorant bliss, thinking that this was the beginning of a new chapter in my life, and that I had left all the negativity and chaos behind me.

Unfortunately, my husband was not on the same page as me. He was wrapped up in the troublesome and toxic ideals of our motherland: that he was less of a man because I was the one in the position of 'power', since he was coming to join me, since I was already established in the UK. By the time he arrived, the honeymoon phase had already begun to fizzle, if not outright dissipated. At any little misunderstanding or disagreement, the first statement he would utter would be something along the lines of "you're behaving like this, because I'm living in your house."

At the time, I was confused, unable to understand what had brought this on, but looking back at it now, it's clear that he felt emasculated, since back in Nigeria, women were subservient to their husbands and typically had little of anything to their name. Nonetheless, since he never articulated his feelings and I was still naïve to certain things in the world, I began walking on eggshells around him, not wanting to incur his anger and feeling it best to placate. So, six months after he arrived he decided that *we* should move out of my house and Milton Keynes, and set up in London, where he was also going to school. Not wanting to spark an argument, I agreed to the move.

Unbeknownst to us at the time of this shift in our lives, another shift was brewing: I was pregnant. A month after we moved to London, I discovered I'd missed my period and went to the hospital for a pregnancy test. It came back positive and I remember the nurse being excited and asking me if I was happy and if the pregnancy was planned. No, the pregnancy was not planned and the jury was still out on if I was happy about it or not.

Nonetheless, terminating it was out of the question. So, I carried the baby to term and after a prolonged labour, I delivered a bouncing baby boy, weighing 7lb 8oz, who we named Ayomide (meaning my joy has come), because we had been in a ghastly motor accident while I was sixteen weeks pregnant, and I thought I was going to lose him.

Fast forward to August 1998 and we were moving into our first home in New Cross as a family: my husband, my now toddler son and I. My husband finished his ACCA exams in December 1998 and became a qualified accountant. He got a part-time job with Newham Council, pending the time he could secure a full-time post. While he was searching, he would say that he was not going to stay in the UK for more than five years, that he would return to Nigeria and live there, but when I pointed out that he had a family here and that moving could be stressful for our son, he would ignore me or dismiss my points.

After a few months of looking, he managed to secure a full-time accounting post with the London Borough of Islington. I thought this would make a difference, that my husband's spiel before had been some manner with which he could exert control over his life. Maybe I should have focused on his words and read more into it. At least that way, we'd both be doing it.

In 1999, I decided that I wanted to further my career by getting a masters degree. When I confided in my husband, I expected that he would give me his full love and support, or at the least, help to make things a little easier for me by helping around the house and with our growing son. Instead, he decided that he too wanted to go for his MSc, and with that in mind, both of us couldn't simultaneously go back to school. He used the stress and pressure I'd been under during my undergraduate course with my job and taking care of a toddler, to convince me to let him go first and once he was done, he would support me with mine. And I believed him.

So, I deferred my admission and did my best to support him, while working and taking care of Ayomide. When he finished in 2000, I reminded him of our agreement but he was quick to change his tune, stating that he meant that he would support me once he had his PhD. At the time, I knew that he was full of it. Now, I realise that he was doing his best to keep me down, so that he could remain on top in our marriage.

I put my foot down and told him that even if he wouldn't support me, I would still further my career. I started my MSc without any support from my husband. I would go to work during the day and study at night. Even over the weekend, in between all the house chores and chaperoning my son to all the activities he was involved in, I studied. At the time, I found the latter surprising, as he seemed to be less and less inclined to do anything with our son, and I couldn't fathom why.

All of a sudden, he stopped taking Ayomide anywhere. He wouldn't go on holiday with us and started to become more and more of a recluse. I couldn't understand why he had begun to change, but now knowing that he was having an affair, it all makes sense. He'd met a lady at his job in

Islington. Her name was Esther, she worked in the canteen, and they became intertwined. I don't know if that was when the affair started, but it definitely began to happen after he came to me, exclaiming that she was in need of a place to stay and that we could provide her with that. None the wiser to his dubious intentions and knowing that we had space, I agreed to let her live with us for six months while she sorted herself out. But six months turned into two years, and all that time, right under my nose, they continued having their affair. Anytime I brought up the topic of her moving out, it would end in a big argument and eventually, I became a shadow of myself in my own home.

In 2003, we celebrated our 10th anniversary – a day that should have been about us and reinforcing our love for one another. Yet Esther decided that she hadn't intruded enough, and after being visibly angry about the whole day, decided to stay away from the house. It was then I started to suspect that there was more to the story, but with no concrete evidence, any accusations would only result in a needless fight. While I was sorting through those feelings, my husband said something along the lines of if your marriage has survived the past five years, there wouldn't be any need for divorce.

Esther eventually managed to secure a job at the Chelsea and Westminster hospital, bought her own house and finally moved out. The joy I felt was immense. My house was once again my own and I didn't have to be a shadow any longer but more importantly, Esther was gone. Yet the joy didn't last long, as I quickly noticed that my husband was coming home from work later and later.

One morning, as I was coming out of the bathroom, I heard him speaking to someone on the phone which ended shortly before I entered the room. When I asked him who he was talking to, he responded with Esther, and when I asked why he was asking her that, he said that it was so that she could get ready. On Saturdays, whenever I wasn't working, Esther would stop by, under the guise of being lonely in her new house. I put up with it for a couple of months before telling her that I was no longer comfortable having her in or around my home, and that since she lived on her own, she should get used to it. She took my words to heart and that was the last I saw of her, but just because I'd stopped her, didn't mean that my husband would stop. Shortly after Esther left the picture, he was introducing a new woman into our lives.

Tolu was introduced as the sister of a close friend of his. She only lived around twenty minutes away from us and so she would be around every so often. My mind didn't immediately see her as a replacement for Esther. Instead, my naivety had me taking him at his word, and believing that if anything were to happen, it would be at her invitation. And so, ever the dutiful and diligent wife, I warned him from getting too close to her. Yet, as was common at this point, my words and warning went unheeded, and soon she was his thinly veiled new girlfriend who was showered with his time and attention.

I remember Mother's Day around 2008, when he decided to take me out to celebrate and for whatever reason, chose to invite Tolu along. At the restaurant, my husband disappeared to make a phone call and wanting to wait for him before ordering food, I opted to get a drink at the bar. It was while I was there that I finally got the proof I needed. I overheard my husband on the phone to someone – presumably a friend – telling them that he was at the restaurant with the *women* in his life. Proof though it was, nothing tangible came of it for a few years. Only the confirmation, the nail in the coffin.

**Gem Under Pressure**
Through all my ordeals, it was difficult at first to see that God was taking me somewhere, and even when death came four different times, in four different forms, God protected me, keeping me so that I can share this story with the world, so that others might learn from it.

After 20 years of being with a narcissist, I finally had my freedom. I remarried and for the past six years, I have found my partner in an old friend of mine that I'd lost contact with. My husband, Sunday Adeolu Laditan, has been my rock, my pillar and has supported me in everything I do. It is together with him that I realised my passion for property, and this gave birth to our property journey.

Despite the challenges and fears that arose with learning something new, we managed to overcome them by ensuring to receive proper training and acquire a mentor to point us in the right direction. I have confidence in everything I do now. Confidence, by my own definition, is that you are brave enough to try new things and as we know, doing new things comes with its own challenges. You must be ready to fall, it's inevitable, but it's not about how many times you fall, rather, it's how many times you get up and continue on. You can do anything no matter how difficult and the abilities which God has given me, because I know that with God all things are possible to those who trust in him.

If I could tell my younger self one thing, it would be this: while you are going through the process of being refined, do not complain. We know gold and diamonds go through high heat and pressure before they become beautiful. So when you are going through your own process, just ask God for the grace and strength as Joseph did when he was going through his own ordeal.

The piece of advice I would give the next generation of female entrepreneurs is believe in yourself and don't let anyone kill your destiny. If you tell people who don't have the same dream as you, you will be met with derision. So, when you have a dream, look for like-minded people who would encourage and challenge you to make that dream come true and invest in yourself and in a mentor.

If you are in an abusive relationship, any kind of relationship, get out of it as soon as possible. So many people have died in an abusive relationship, leaving a void that is impossible to fill. And since abuse comes in so many forms other than physical – verbal, mental, financial and emotional – just because they don't lay a hand on you, doesn't mean that you should subject yourself to that abuse. Do not wait for anyone's' approval to tell you who you are or your worth. Believe in yourself and take any necessary step to achieve your goals and ambition.

## About Me

My name is Olufunmilola Abimbola Olatunde and I am a biomedical scientist in my circular job screening cervical smears, detecting precancerous cells in women at the NNUH. I am also a property investor based in Norfolk and I recently won the Traveller Review Award 2023 on booking.com. I decided to feature in the QIB book as it's the best platform for me to tell my story and to encourage women out there that whatever they go through in life, God has a hand in it and He is building them for every next step and stage of their lives.

I acknowledge my mum Mrs A R Olatunde for the way she has trained and brought me up to be a strong woman, my son Ayomide Olufemi Olubode for all his perseverance and the encouragement he gave and, in dedication to the memory of my loving father Mr Ezekiel Olaniyi Olatunde and cousin Mr Kunle Oderinu, who had gone to glory for all their encouragement throughout my life. To my encouraging husband Mr Sunday Adeolu Laditan, for all the support he has given me so far, he has brought out the brightness in me again.

# Counselling In Confidence

### Jaimini Ravalia
Pluralist Psychotherapeutic Counsellor
Progressive Therapies

"Sometimes belief is all that's needed, the rest takes care of itself" – Anonymous

Yikes! I had just turned forty-four on New Year's Eve and I welcomed 2023 with open arms. In 2022, I was the most badass boldest brunette I have ever had to be! More on that later, but I will say one thing for now, there was a point where my confidence was rock bottom and non-existent.

Most of us go through life believing that we'll reach a point of absolute certainty and then it'll be a straightforward path mapped out to follow. Sorry to break it to you, there is no such thing as absolute certainty. I can say *that* with total confidence!!! In fact, the only thing 'certain' in life is change, so why do we resist it? Change happens consistently to all of us but for some reason people begrudge going through it.

Change can be challenging but it doesn't have to spell death and destruction! I know, that sounds a little dramatic – I have witnessed people behave as though any change means the end of the world. They think of it as a problem, therefore feeling out of control. So instead of regaining control and composure, their thoughts govern their behaviour and before you know it, they are testing the tenacity of their confidence. When I think about my own experiences of confidence, I know that even in my darkest hour (and I've come through a few of those) I have the spirit to be forward-looking. I don't want my life to pass me by. I wake up every single day grateful for another day with the opportunity to accomplish anything I set my mind to.

I do wonder if the ability to accept change readily has much to do with being a psychologist. I have been training the beautiful mind since I was sixteen years old and I have never stopped learning. There is always something new to understand and I can confidently read your mind while you stand there in front of me unsuspecting of what I can hear you actually saying! Just kidding!!!!

Actually, I can read behaviour, body language, facial gestures and non-verbal cues that give me clues about what someone might be thinking and feeling especially when it contradicts what they are saying.

As you read my chapter, I want you to consider my confidence in layers. The top layer of confidence is what everyone perceives and is the persona I put out to the world, the middle layer is my lifestyle – where I travel, what qualifications I have, where I live, my job, my career, the car I drive and the house I live in. Lastly, the inner layer – my core confidence – is the relationship with myself, my truth, my conscience. I want you to begin noticing these layers in yourself, taking note of where you think you could further develop your confidence.

**Adventure Awaits!**

I want to take you back to when I turned twenty-two. I felt like I had the world at my feet, setting off to New York for New Year's Eve (my birthday) and feeling so blooming confident that I would not have guessed that it could disappear one day. Like many twenty-two year olds, I thought confidence would be a thing that develops with a steady incline, and once you've got it, that's it, qualification in confidence complete! In New York City I had a great first time abroad with my cousins. It's an incredible end to 2000 and the best start to 2001.

Upon my return, I finished my Bachelor of Science undergraduate degree in Psychology and Women's Studies, all achieved with Honours which holds more academic recognition than a general BSc. I'm not bragging, just setting the scene for how confident I was feeling in my abilities to step forward and make some important career decisions. So, what does an academic do next? Study some more of course! I studied one further year for accreditation and I then decided I had had enough of studying… in England.

Studying abroad is super expensive. I couldn't go to Europe because of the language barriers but a friend and I figured Australia was the least complicated destination to gain a qualification and had the best exchange rate at the time. It's 2004 and I am literally still umming and ahhing about my future specialism within psychology. I have a passion to work with children and young people and I even coached tennis one summer with an elite coaching club who were constantly scouting for Wimbledon.

I earned a killing in one summer for minimal working hours but I didn't feel the satisfaction I thought I would. I suppose, the sports psychologist in me didn't spark and leap out of bed, not even for the money. The other path to explore was an educational psychologist and I would find plenty of children and young people in education sectors. Bingo! That's what I'll do. My friend and I set off to Perth, Australia for a year to achieve a postgraduate certification in secondary education (basically a teaching qualification was necessary for the educational psychologist route).

Perth was amazing but I was homesick for the first six months and I wasn't feeling particularly confident about my choice to study the PGCE. I have zero interest in teaching, so it was a real passion killer to say the least. At the university, my professors were genuinely interested in me and at first couldn't understand why I had bothered to come to the other side of the world for a basic PGCE. Once I explained, they moved mountains for me!

Instead of teaching in schools for two terms, I was allowed to shadow an educational psychologist. This is unheard of in the UK! I was so incredibly grateful. What it taught me was that anything is possible and if you don't ask the question, you will never know the answer. At twenty-four, this was an 'aha' moment that really did make all the difference to my existence.

Anyway, besides it being the best thing I ever did, and to cut a long story short, I never even got to qualify as an educational psychologist in the end. The other thing I learned was that the role of educational psychologist in the UK was vastly different to the role I had become accustomed to in Perth. I didn't fancy being stuck behind a desk pushing assessment papers across it. I wanted to truly make a difference. I had no idea what I was going to do next. I was feeling like Australia was a waste of a year as I didn't want to teach – and I didn't even want to teach psychology.

I am fascinated with human behaviour and by now, my own behaviour was beginning to spell trouble. When I returned home after that year, I was so low, so sad and so moneyless. The determination and confidence that I could make a difference to one young person at a time was fading fast. I kept thinking how I have ended up like this! I questioned myself over and over, I wanted to give up, I was so frustrated with my life! I didn't feel worthy to be in the field of psychology anymore. I would rather hide away and not be seen. This was a poignant time in my journey as a female trying so hard to keep my ambitions alive, I could feel my self-belief fading away and my self-esteem disappearing.

My dad could see that I needed something, so he spoke to his friend who offered me an office job. Well, I had to do something! The office was at the end of my road which was approximately 30 feet from my house. I did that job for six weeks and soon enough after the first few weeks, when I'd come home for lunch, I would feel like I was ready to pull my

135

hair out. I hated it! It gave me the assurance that I needed to do something that I loved. So much so that I volunteered with Barnardo's children's charity just so I could feel my spark again. Money and earning was important but so was doing what I love. I chose my relationship with myself in that moment. The pain of doing anything else other than what I felt was 'my calling' was the reason for turning it around for myself. My core confidence was my driver, my fuel, my inspiration. Thanks to my dad, who unknowingly, had used reverse psychology to help me find my way again.


**The Chelsea Years**
Finally in 2006, I started my first proper long-term contracted job with a hospital school with four very separate unique sites. I remember feeling very nervous, my confidence was shaken at the core because previously I had no luck finding a job that I thought I would love. It was very important to me to do what I loved, to serve others and make even the smallest difference as opposed to change the world.

I didn't know what to expect in Chelsea and my weeks were split between two sites. I didn't feel settled at either site and what was I really being asked to do most of the time, yep, you got it, teach or assist teaching!

The saving grace was the hospital school was based in the paediatric ward so I could be working at a bedside, in isolation or a cohort of young people from the community who had fallen through the security net of mainstream education. Don't get me wrong, mental health for children and young people was high on the agenda at every hospital school site but my aim was to gain experience with working with young people so I could pursue the educational psychologist route further – at least that's what the British Psychological Society (BPS) wanted at the time. As I settled into my role, I was to go through another setback, the BPS decided to make further changes to the educational psychologist role and I no longer felt connected to it which triggered my sense of worth.

The more I settled, the more I could see the gaps in mental health support that the children and young people at the hospital schools did not have access to. I naturally began to fill that gap, become their confidant and safe space where they could share their most vulnerable self. I experienced a profound shift in my understanding of myself. I started to feel more confident with every conversation I had the privilege of influencing. I didn't care what my job title was or what my salary was, I just knew I was helping and that was more than enough. I had found my dream job! I was to become a therapist but – and it was a BIG but – at the time, it would have meant more studying, so I decided to wait. Later, I was advised that my age would go against me, so don't bother! Seriously! I was heartbroken and I didn't believe in myself enough to even try.

Within the hospital school the hierarchical structure existed like it would in any school. I was at the bottom of this hierarchy. That didn't help me feel good about myself but a select few individuals that I worked closely with could see what I was trying to create. Eventually, what I created was a mentoring role that didn't previously exist at the hospital school. I proposed it to my line manager and head teacher and they were very supportive of the plan. I had found a qualification (I know what you're thinking, she's studying again!) that supported mentoring in mental health, and then I found another trainer in statistical analysis to teach me to analyse the data I would collate from the mentoring so I could prove that it was making a difference, a positive difference, to young people's lives.

I then went on to propose that every site that needed a mentor should have one, and it was approved along with a team of three mentors at my site because that is where the greatest demand was. When Ofsted came to inspect the hospital school, it was one of my proudest moments. At first, they didn't want to speak to me because they thought I'd just talk at them about what I had achieved. They had no idea about the measurable data I had been collating. But I insisted on speaking to them (even my head teacher was surprised, no one actually ever wants to speak to Ofsted!). They were very impressed with my initiative and I felt truly outstanding (along with the school's rating) that day because that's what it was all about! Not being rich or famous but making a positive difference to one young person at a time and having recognition for the hard work helps too.

Wow! Can you imagine what this was doing for my confidence!? Nothing else mattered. I worked so hard to create this, and when I asked myself why did I do this? The answer was simple. When I was at school, I went through a lot of painful experiences, such as toxic friendships, bullying and to top it all off, my upbringing was unreasonably strict that I had no one to confide in, no one to understand me, no one to talk to. I experienced shame, embarrassment and guilt throughout my adolescent years and this was not okay. I felt worthless throughout my school life but nobody knew that but me. My core relationship with myself was in bad shape and continued to be throughout college, university and Australia. It didn't matter where I went, my core truth came with me.

This is where my persona really played a significant part in stopping anyone knowing what was going on under the surface. I became excellent at hiding my true feelings but was well-known for being cheeky and having a big smile. I have big brown eyes too, so all-in-all they served as a great cover up.

**Present Day**
Skip to the future – I married, had three children, qualified as a psychotherapeutic counsellor, divorced and set-up my private practice. The latter two happened in the last twelve months of writing this chapter. My marriage was like being in a Bollywood movie, some singing and dancing but with so much melodrama, it was suffocating me. I had to leave the melodrama behind and it is why I had to be the badass boldest brunette version of myself I have ever had to be. I didn't know

I had it in me. I certainly didn't feel brave or courageous, I found myself on the cold hard floor most days just trying to muddle through, trying to make sense of my married life and what was to become of me. I was terrified and most of all the levels of anxiety I felt were seriously high. I experienced debilitating levels of anxiety, to the point where I would spend hours crying or unable to move. I have three children to take care of and as I think back now, they were my only reason for getting myself out of bed. They needed me to live when I thought I couldn't take any more.

Motherhood strips us down to be the most vulnerable parts of ourselves as women, yet vulnerability is not a weakness. It takes a great deal of courage to be vulnerable. I have felt this vulnerability at various other points in my life but the early experiences of motherhood the second time around compelled me to become single minded. I had twins in 2015 and a three year old, which meant a total career break and no space in my schedule for part-time work. It took me two years after having the twins to resurface as a human being, those years were challenging to say the least.

The first thing I did was find an online course, when the children slept, I studied! I achieved a qualification in cognitive behavioural therapy and that was it, the passion was back, the spark felt so good, learning and growth felt like I was me again. I found the online study world appealing, but to be clinically trained I needed a university qualification. So, I signed up for a postgraduate diploma in psychotherapy and counselling with a local university. I became that mum who was readily available as mum by day and studied late nights and very early mornings to meet the deadlines of assignments. I wanted what any career driven ambitious woman wants – a fruitful career! I wanted my independence, I wanted my life to look like it was mine and I wanted my path to be my own, not to follow the footprints left before me.

**Therapy**

My clients are young people and adults. I have yet to meet an adult who has not experienced some form of trauma during their childhood or adolescence that still impacts on their adult life. I am in the business of helping people self-actualise, that basically means I guide my clients towards their core truth. It's my dream job but I didn't take the straight road there and for that I am grateful. I could not have imagined that one day I would be running my very own private practice let alone running a business. I suppose I had a naïve preconceived idea that people in business just want to make money. Since being in business, I have met many wonderful people who want to make a difference, who have value and purpose to share with humanity and to help improve humanity.

I have worked so damn hard to get to where I am today, but what I wanted to highlight in my story here, is that my confidence wasn't always rock solid. Especially throughout the Chelsea years, my confidence fluctuated immensely and yet I made some great changes that still live on seven years after I left.

My whole life took on a major change 12 months ago but I still managed to create a business and keep myself and my children as safe as I could. I did the best that I could. The point is this, your confidence is in your belief about yourself and what you are doing for others. Yes, my subconscious governed what I created and what I wanted for others was what I didn't have for myself.

The business world was a scary world. I had my mentors telling me that I need to be visible to raise my status and authority. I'm thinking, but I'm happy in my modesty getting on with what I do and doing it quietly, that suits me. It took me totally by surprise that I should be so worried about business-related social media posts or being interviewed or podcasting. I had to really look at myself.

I knew I had to change this. I'm not afraid of change but this was particularly disconcerting. As I searched my unconscious mind to figure out what was at play here, I came across a core belief that 'I am not good enough', ergo imposter syndrome. We all have the little imposter alert every now and again, it's completely normal. It's also not worth ignoring as it has a nasty habit of becoming bigger than it deserves to be. So, I recommend you sit with it, unwrap it layer by layer and understand its origins.

Mine came from mixed messaging throughout my adolescence stemming from my upbringing so I developed a great deal of self-doubt. So much so, that when my parents told me something was not for me or wasn't the right time for me, I would believe them. Once I understood where my core belief derived from, I stopped feeding it. That is to say my awareness for it grew stronger and I stopped integrating information that reinforced the core belief as mine. I rejected it!

To be the most badass boldest brunette version of myself I have needed to rediscover every part of myself. I knew that's how far I needed to go to live up to my values of being authentic, congruent and empathetic. I have forgiven the versions of myself I have had to be in order to get through some truly horrid periods of my life. I have no doubt that I will be a version of myself in my future that I can be proud of because I am still willing to be vulnerable and courageous, they move together hand-in-hand.

Success is important to me but not necessarily in the monetary sense. I had a 'penny dropping' moment in the middle of a session with a client. I was listening to her tell me about her situation when I realised, she may as well be describing me. I could feel the anxiety rising within me and I was questioning my courage to hold myself to the values I hold so closely. This client had no idea what she had evoked, but I am glad she did. My values live at the core of my truth with confidence and they're all wrapped up in the core beliefs I chose for myself and not the beliefs that were projected onto me.

I'm in the business of helping people self-actualise. If I didn't attempt to self-actualise for myself, would I even be a 'good enough' therapist?

I'm not seeking perfectionism, I am bound to make mistakes. But fake is one thing I'm not willing to be! All this really means is that there comes a time in a woman's life where she has accumulated layers that no longer serve her, time to shed those layers. Sometimes, those shedding layers are painful and sometimes they are not. I am bound by my ethics that no harm should come to those who come to me for treatment and solutions. They seek their true selves, they come with the confidence that I too have done the inner work or else what do I know about consciously living any more than the textbooks I qualified from?

Starting my business in my dream job has been fun to figure out. I haven't always felt assured about the money side of it, all I knew is that my subconscious voice had become louder. The quiet little good girl needed expression, the woman I had adapted into wanted more for herself and for others. I wanted to be at home for my children, I didn't want to work for someone else. I wanted my conditions of worth to be my own and to transcend me to my higher purpose.

I have had too many people over the years dictate what my life should look like. It didn't feel right, I didn't feel aligned with who I was.

Within my journey so far, I have transformed myself physically, mentally, spiritually and intellectually. Everything about me has been subject to change. As I write this chapter, I have no doubt that more change is inevitable but the path of rediscovering myself, my core confidence is fully present and the other layers give me a poised stand point to ground me while I newly navigate the world of business and entrepreneurship.

You can do whatever you set your mind to. Your mindset and self-belief are key to how confidently you step out into the business world. Your core confidence, your relationship with yourself holds the courage, spirit and determination, and will strengthen with you as you desire growth both in business and outside of business. The persona and lifestyle layers are interchangeable and more conveniently adaptable.

A beautiful friend of mine gave me the words in a quote at the top of this chapter. Those words were given to me when I needed them the most and I hope those words reach you too.

## About Me

I am a qualified pluralist psychotherapeutic counsellor, speaker and co-author. I have worked as a mental health practitioner for 20+ years with children, young people and adults. My approach is pluralistic which means I essentially believe that one 'school of thought' cannot help everyone. Therefore, a multidimensional understanding of The Self is what I hope to deliver to advocate self-love, self-development and the journey towards your core truth.

My mission is to normalise mental health for ALL and to remove the stigma that has been associated with mental health problems and labelling. We aren't our problems, the problem is the problem. We all have a medical professional to turn to, so we ought to have a mental health professional to reach out to as well.

I wanted to take this opportunity to share my story because I want to be able to reach you and hopefully help you to understand *confidence* and that the different layers of confidence are all relevant to each of us. No matter where you come from culturally, nationally or geographically, confidence is an integral part of the systems of belief that we all carry. My hope is that after reading my chapter you are able to identify with your confidence and strengthen it. My wish is that you're able to be greater than you are and evolve.

I dedicate this chapter to my parents, Shanti and Jasu Ravalia, who have always supported my academic journey with love and respect for the study of the mind and human behaviour. Without their support, I would not have accomplished as much as I have today. For that I am truly grateful.

# Be Strong And Courageous

### Olu Famakin
Co Founder
Jeda Relocation

"Confidence is to trust and self-confidence is having trust in one's self" – Unknown

I am a property investor and business owner but this hasn't always been the case. I did all the 'go to school, get a job, carve a career' path, but I realised after almost two decades in my career that there is nothing like a job for life or job security. This is an illusion to keep people in bondage, stifling creativity and eventually becoming a society of burnt out individuals.

I was born in London but at the age of one returned to Nigeria with my parents who had been studying in the UK. As the youngest of three girls at that time, I was brought up in a culture that favoured boys. I didn't want to be a girl. I felt I was disadvantaged because I was. I even 'hated God' for making me a girl.

Success in our culture at the time was to go to school, be the best, always come first – second was never good enough. My parents would say, "The person that came first doesn't have two heads, why couldn't you come first?" My parents encouraged us to study hard and gave us a good education. They wanted us to make something of ourselves so we would become independent. Education is a gift, it opens up your horizon. I am forever grateful for this.

Coming back to society's view about girls. A relative once said to my mother, "Do you think you have children?" despite her having three girls at that time. As a girl, I had to prove to the naysayers that I was worth the education I had been given by those that believed in me.

While growing up, the great role models around me were my father, my mother and grandmother. My mother and grandmother were very industrious. Despite having a job, my mother also had small businesses while my grandmother had small businesses into her later years providing a service to the community. My grandmother was well known and loved in her community. She was a woman of great wisdom.

My mother always said to us, "A woman must have her career to be able to stand on her own and not depend on any man." This is so true but many cultures around the world still don't think it is worth educating women. Our environment can shape us either positively or negatively.

**School Years**
At school I had a chemistry teacher (Miss Abiri) who made me fall in love with the subject.

Unknown to me then, this would define my career path. The year I was supposed to take my GCSE exams, I was injured in a car accident and was in hospital until a few weeks before my exams. I was still in pain but I had to return to school. On returning back to school, my father asked for my exams to be deferred to the following year so as to retake the school year that I had missed. I wasn't very happy with this decision but it proved to be a blessing in disguise. I gained five GCSE including chemistry which I needed to pursue further education.

The next step in my journey was to apply to university. My preferred course was pharmacy. I did the university entrance exams twice but my scores were not enough to be considered to study pharmacy. Sometimes you might have to change direction but never change your goal or vision. While waiting for the university admission, I decided to keep studying so I registered at the polytechnic for a course in applied chemistry.

While at the polytechnic, I had to submit a piece of coursework to one of my male lecturers but as I was about to leave, he asked me which part of the country my family was from. I told him Ibadan which is in the west. He looked at me in shock and said, "People from your area don't pursue education and not even girls for that matter." I was mortified. What a stereotype! What prejudice!

Sometimes, because of what people say or what people will say we don't pursue our dreams and as such stifle the greatness within us. Don't listen to the unbelievers. Believe in yourself.

This made me even more determined to succeed.

I still had the goal of going to university, so I attempted the entrance exams for the third time and this time, I decided to study biochemistry. I passed and gained admission for a four year course in the subject. After the first and second time of trying and failing the exams, I could have given up. Not everything at university was rosy, I passed most of my courses, failed a few and had to resit them.

In the third year, my mother was made redundant at work. It was tough but there was no chance of either of us giving up. She started a small business and with the additional support of my father as well, I finished my course and graduated.


**Back To The Beginning**
After graduation I returned back to the UK. Since leaving the country as a toddler, I had only visited once as a teenager and now I was back in my twenties. It was a big culture shock.

I arrived at the end of January. On the second day of my arrival, it started to snow. I had never seen snow, it looked so beautiful but it was extremely cold. Coming from a temperature of 30 degrees to below zero, I did not venture outside for two weeks.

On the day I decided to go out after much persuasion, I ended up on my backside having slipped on the snow. What a rude awakening. Apart from being so cold, it seemed like it was constantly dark and barely any daylight existed. This made me question if the sun ever shone in the UK. I wanted to go back home so badly. I was finding it difficult to adjust to all the changes.

I am so glad I held on, and having people around me, my sister and uncle that kept encouraging me that it would get better. Surrounding ourselves with positive people that will support us, encourage us and carry us when we need it is very important.

Spring arrived and my outlook changed. Seasons come and seasons go, nothing lasts forever.

Now what was the next step for me? I started to apply for jobs that I thought I qualified for but nothing was forthcoming. There were obstacles left, right and centre. It was either, "Oh you are over qualified" or "Sorry you are under qualified" or "You don't have experience."

I found a job as a cleaner, then catering assistant and later a sales assistant. These jobs gave me skills such as working with the public, team working and also experience of working in the UK. My uncle also said to me, "You have to work twice as hard as your White counterparts."

I persevered with these jobs and then got the opportunity to retrain for six months gaining IT skills. In those days, it was word processing using typewriters and word processors with the aim of getting a job in an office. During this course, I got talking to the tutor and director and told him about myself and that I was a university graduate. He looked at me and said, "We have to help you, you can do better than this."

Ralph took it upon himself to get me whatever funding I was entitled to. I had no idea what it was or where to get the relevant information. I received funding for a Masters, passed the interview and then completed the year's course.

**Daily Grind**
As long as I could remember, I was interested in research. I started to apply as a research assistant, sent application after application but the answer was always no thank you. After a while, my sister who was a biomedical scientist in cytology suggested I follow the same career path but in a different discipline. I started to apply and got offered two trainee positions within the space of two weeks. I had the choice to train in haematology or biochemistry. I chose biochemistry.

I started my training and at the same time doing some more courses at university to compliment the degrees I had. After my training, I applied for my state registration and I became a qualified biomedical scientist. I was happy now, as I saw a clear career path. As we are taught by society, you start at the bottom of the career ladder and you work your way up.

A year after qualifying, I got married and we started a family. Not long after having my second child, I realised that having a full-time job and bringing up two children wasn't a piece of cake. I decided working part-time was the answer but it didn't leave enough at the end of the month. This was the only way I knew to continue with my career and take care of my family. Truth be told, it was comfortable and I carried on until I decided I needed a change.

After eleven years, I realised that if I wanted to continue climbing the corporate ladder I had to move from my comfort zone. Fast forward to lots of applications and interviews later, and I got offered two senior positions within a few weeks of each other.

Now the dilemma was a) get the whole family to move because of my job or b) travel two hours to and from work everyday. I chose the second option.

I had to work full-time, still had my family responsibilities and a four-hour journey every day. When you have to do something, you will find a way. Along with the support of those around me, life and work carried on. I enjoyed what I was doing, gaining different skills and experience. Working with people with different personalities, and especially leading a team, had its own challenges. It became apparent to me that people are people everywhere, and all I had to do was look deep within my family structure, nuclear or extended and draw from my experiences of dealing with them. Above all, it was to treat people with respect and with empathy and not just numbers, whether team members or clients.

Have you ever felt that there must be more to life than what you are currently doing? This was how I felt in 2016.

**Burn Out**

I was on my way to work. This wasn't new, I had been doing this same commute for twelve years. An hour and a half into my journey, I got off the train to go and get the bus. This was supposed to be the last leg of the journey.

Upon getting to the bus stop, rather than getting on the bus, I went back to the train station and kept going around the same one mile radius going forwards and backwards on the train back to the bus stop but not continuing on the direction to work.

After doing this for about an hour, I asked myself, "What are you doing?" It was like I had been in a trance. I went back to the train station, got on a train and went back home and slept for two weeks. This was my burn out. I was physically and mentally exhausted. I decided enough was enough.

After two weeks, I went back to work with my letter of resignation in my hand and handed it to my manager. I was ready to resign but he read it and said, "What can we do to help you?"

At this point, I didn't have a plan, I just knew something had to give. Pain can make you overreact sometimes but in business, you need to be focused, level-headed and have a plan.

My manager had empathy with my situation and this gave me the courage to request to work part-time which reduced how many days I was doing this long commute. This then gave me the push to look for work closer to home which reduced my commute time even more. Despite this new job and reduced commute time, I still didn't feel fulfilled. I was constantly tired, stressed and didn't feel in control of my life.

I knew getting another job was not the answer. I wanted to be able to feel like I had a choice and in control of my life. A couple of years before, my friend and colleague (Marion) gave me a book to read, Rich Dad, Poor Dad by Robert Kiyosaki. This book opened my eyes to a different system. The idea of working until retirement wasn't going to cut it. By retirement, the government won't have anything left in the pension pot because we are all living longer, this was not sustainable.

It showed me that if I wanted to be in control of my life, to be able to do what I want, when I want, I needed a new strategy. Being an employee will not give me this freedom, only by being a business owner and investor would I be able to achieve the level of freedom that I wanted.

This prompted me to start looking into property investing again. See, I had tried this a couple of years ago but due to some bad decisions I made, I failed and rather than analyse and assess what went wrong, I told myself the system didn't work and threw in the towel. Truth be told, it wasn't the system that was broken, I had lost confidence in myself.

This was back in 2007. I had gone on a three day property course and thought I knew all that I needed to know. How on earth did I think this was going to be a walk in the park?

During this time, buying property was all the rage – in adverts on TV, on posters, everywhere was about buying abroad in warmer climates. I went to a property exhibition and there was this company with glossy magazines, posters, including convincing sales people selling the idea of buying in Spain. I got sucked in, did everything that I was taught not to do, I was chasing the "shiny penny". I didn't seek any advice from any mentors because I thought I was now qualified to invest in property. In January 2008, I persuaded my husband and we went to Spain with this company. All expenses were paid by them apart from the flight, and we spent the weekend looking at properties.

By the Sunday, we had paid a holding deposit on an off-plan property and were excited. We returned home and on the Monday paid another large deposit. For anyone that is old enough to remember 2008, there was a global recession and the property market crashed. Many people lost their money especially in Spain and the rest of Europe.

For two years, the company kept reassuring us that they were still on track and everything was going well until we stopped hearing from them. Shortly after this, we learnt the company had gone into liquidation and we lost all our deposit. While a novice like me lost money, savvy property investors and business people made money.

The lessons I learnt from this were that half-baked education is not good enough, never buy in a market that you don't know, do your homework, do your due diligence, ask the experts and always have a mentor that knows what they are doing. Also, remember: all that glitters is not gold.

The experience shook me to the core and I gave in to the fear of failure and went back to what was safe. I went back to my job and continued with my crazy hours. Despite trying to rise further in my career, it seemed like I had reached the ceiling. I was becoming more and more disheartened because I knew I wasn't growing and that I had more to give. I was only going through the emotions. Going to work everyday, coming home, going to sleep and then back the next day and repeating it all over again. Don't get me wrong, my career had served me well up until now but every time I thought, is this what I will be doing until retirement? I knew the answer was no – even though I was scared of the unknown. If I didn't change, nothing was going to change.

**The Change**

In 2021, during the pandemic, I decided this was my time for change after attending a property course on Zoom. This sparked a long lost interest in me. I knew I had to learn from my past mistakes.

This time, I knew I have to learn from the best, follow proven systems and have a mentor who knows what they are talking about and are walking the walk. As my mother always said, "Learn from those who know better than you."

As soon as lockdown was over, I started my in-person training. This hasn't been easy, working full-time and creating a business, just as we spend time studying and learning in mainstream school, learning about property is continuous. I've had to be coachable and adaptable.

Property relocation is a people business whether dealing with clients, agents or landlords. I found dealing with agents quite challenging because their systems are built around residential tenants and not so much companies. Once agents understood who we were and what we were about, it became easier to work with them and provide them and their clients (landlords and tenants) with a great service.

Learning to trust myself and my instincts has also proved invaluable. Also, being part of a community of like minded people and motivated people such as my business partner Hina, has helped me. Our visions and goals align, we have been able to achieve a lot together. What is that saying: two heads are better than one.

Being an entrepreneur is very different from being an employee. There are many skills I knew I needed but the biggest thing for me has been changing my mindset. Working on my mindset is a daily thing. To do something different, I have to think differently. People that have achieved greatness such as Einstein, Bill Gates and Elon Musk might be regarded as eccentric but they all went against the norm.

As an employee you're given objectives to work towards, you have to follow the employer's vision, you don't have a say in it. You cannot be creative or take risks. As an entrepreneur, I needed to know who I am, what I want, what my message is and who I would like to serve.

Before I could be of service to anyone, I needed to heal myself. Healing can be instantaneous or gradual. Firstly, I had to ask for forgiveness for ever doubting The Potter (my maker, God). I needed to be myself and not what anyone says I should be or want me to be.

I am unique and created for a purpose. We all have gifts inside of us. Walk in yours and don't be envious of others. When we are ready to receive, opportunities will present themselves. One of these opportunities came when I attended Reign Like A Queen. I saw women that were championing women. Society has taught us that as women, to be in business or to rise to the top of your profession, you have to be brutal – you have to behave like a man. Remember you can be whatever you want to be, you can break barriers: they are meant to be broken but in all this, stay true to who you are.

I would like to thank Queens In Business for giving me the opportunity to share my story. I am hoping to inspire other women to their greatness.

## About Me

Born in London, raised in Lagos and now living in the South East of England. I am married and have a son and a daughter. I am the Co-Founder of JEDA Relocation, we provide our clients with a comfortable home from home accommodation.

I have worked as a biomedical scientist for the past twenty-eight years in different hospital laboratories. During this time, I have realised that whatever job you do it is always about the people you work with and not necessarily the job itself. Most of our adult life is spent in the workplace. As such, it is important to nurture work relationships as well as other relationships.

When everything is said and done, it is that which matters because you never know where you will meet again. The world is a small place.

One of my philosophies is to treat people well so when next you meet them, you will be eager to say hello and not have to cross the road with your head bowed.

I am grateful to Queens In Business for this opportunity to share my story with you the reader, and I hope this will give you the confidence to go and achieve your dreams. I dedicate this chapter to all those that have been my support along the way, my mother Adelaide, my husband Valentine, my sister Lola who is always an inspiration to me. My children Dami and Toni, my business partner Hina, Ralph my coach and Marion Rowe (for the lovely book).

# Return To Yourself

## Christina Chalmers
Founder
Body Intelligence
Sports Therapy and Wellness Solutions

"Self-confidence is a skill, and like all skills, you can get better at it if you put in the work" – Unknown

At six years old, I began gymnastics classes. I loved everything about it! The energy, jumping around and learning new skills. Everything was so much fun. It suited me better than ballet and tap dancing, which I'd tried the previous year.

I progressed through my badges and was recommended to move up from my Saturday morning class to the local club. Our main apparatus was floor and vault, including the discipline of sports acrobatics as it was known back then (now known as acrobatic gymnastics, womens pairs and groups).

After some time, I was asked to be a base for pairs, and later on trios. Being taller than your average gymnast, the ability to physically support others came quite naturally to me. I also quite enjoyed working with other gymnasts on the floor, I felt less alone and less exposed when compared to performing solo. I was soon training six hours a week, practising for competitions and summer displays.

As I got older, I was often asked to assist younger gymnasts in class, something I enjoyed doing. I took my Assistant Coaches exam at fifteen years old and passed, although validation had to be delayed until my sixteenth birthday. This meant I could be financially rewarded for my efforts.

At eighteen I took my Class 4 (Full) Coaches exam, allowing me to teach classes of 20 children in gymnastics and have assistants work with me. Again, I loved it! Gymnastics was ingrained within me. I used to eat, sleep and breathe it. Having grown up with it, the confidence was there by the bucket load, without me even knowing it.

I can remember being asked by one of our younger gymnasts at a competition, "Why aren't you nervous?" to which I replied, "Well, I've done lots of these, so it's okay, I know what to expect, I will be nervous later, but only a few minutes before I'm on the floor. You will be alright too."

Throughout my time in gymnastics, there were other confident people around me. Anytime that anyone was trying to achieve a new skill or felt nervous, whether it was in class or at a competition, there were clubmates and coaches who cheered you on, supported and encouraged you. There was a lot of positive energy you could draw from.

Gymnastics also allowed me to be creative in many ways, in choreographing our competition routines, but also in classes creating exercises for the members which were fun but allowed them to progress and achieve more advanced skills. Each child is different, sometimes as a coach you need to find an alternative exercise for the child to achieve the result you are looking for.

Gymnastics made me feel amazing. School however, in my experience, was a different matter. If you stood out, excelled at something, looked different, or didn't fit in, you were targeted. You might be praised by a teacher but then you were teased and taunted by some of your classmates. I wanted to fit in but at the same time, I just wanted to be me. Understanding my own uniqueness, learning to be me and accepting myself was to come much later in life. For now, I didn't want to be seen, I wanted to blend into the background and go unnoticed like the little girl on the stage in pre-school who shuffled to hide herself behind the curtain. Now you can't see me.

Throughout my life I've often had difficulty with self-expression. I hated having parts in school assembly. Reading passages out loud in class, I would pray for the bell to ring before it got to my turn. My nervousness would grow and grow, heart thumping, feeling like I was physically shaking. I'd stutter and stammer, fall over the words, provoking laughter, sniggering and mocking, and be left feeling embarrassed. One day, my history teacher questioned me at the end of class, "Can you read?" he asked, in a gruff tone (and most likely out of concern). My reply, "Yes I can read, I just don't like reading out in class." He nodded.

When I was young, I feared being told off or shouted at, it would render me silent. Words would seem to get stuck in my throat. The only response I had, would be to cry. At numerous times in my life, I have felt challenged and lacked the support that I needed at work, during important exams, and at school where (on a couple of occasions) I had been hauled up in front of the class and made an example of as a bad student. At the time, I chose to suppress these incidents only for them to resurface later in life.

**Finding My Path**

Back in 1997 I completed my first Sports Therapy qualification. The Level 3 Diploma course combined everything I loved about sport and the human body. I had enjoyed the course so much that I wanted to know more and take my studies further.
I began researching how to get into physiotherapy. Admissions tutors had informed me that I would need to have A Levels or equivalent in the sciences, in particular human biology or biology.

Academically I struggled and didn't achieve the required grades. Every time I took a course, comments about more education, and when I'm going to get a job came from friends and family. Eventually, I took an access course to get myself to the right level and succeeded. I also set about getting some experience with physios, and for six months I observed treatments and assisted in the hydrotherapy pool at Burrswood – a lovely facility in the East Sussex countryside.

I made three rounds of applications through UCAS to try to gain a place on a physiotherapy degree. In the year 2000, my final application cycle, I decided that this year, I was going to university or never going at all. So I accepted a place on the sports science degree that ran alongside a sports therapy degree with the intention to switch courses. It wasn't easy to make the transition, but I was determined to make it happen and knew this was the path I wanted to follow.

My practical skills always exceeded my academic skills. I did well in both written and practical assignments. I loved the studies, discovering how the human body works and what to do with it when things go awry. However, I was to experience my first major setback when I failed a compulsory unit for my degree. I wasn't the only student in this situation.

At my viva for my dissertation, I fared much better. One of my tutors encouraged me to get my insurance for practice. I nodded but the belief in myself just wasn't there. I graduated but was consumed with survival. I needed to pay my rent and bills, so I jumped back into my catering job, telling my boss to "give me everything you've got, I am broke!" – having already had a couple of parental bailouts, just so I could pay my rent.

So, I got my insurance, all ready to practise. Now comes the tricky part. I started applying for jobs, trying to get a break in my industry. Nervous at interviews, I was rejected from every single one. With a number of reasons given, notably: "you don't have enough experience" and one where I was categorically told: "you won't cope" even though the complete pay structure had just been explained to me. All I wanted was the chance to try. But for now, I had to survive, and it was back to the day job.

**Olympic Dreams**

In 2005, we were awarded the Olympics, the games would be coming to London in 2012! How amazing is that?! The very next day we were plunged into chaos as the 7/7 attacks took place. I had gone through the London Underground around fifty minutes before the events began. At this time, I was working in a government building on Whitehall. We were locked down, nobody was allowed in or out, which meant for a very busy day in our restaurant and shop.

At the end of our day, we were allowed out on foot, no transport was running anywhere in the centre of London. I walked with a colleague across town in the strange, eerie silence to which London is not accustomed. We had been given directions that buses were running north bound from close to Kings Cross.

A few days later, as things slowly returned to normal, I visited Trafalgar Square, the scene of jubilation and celebration when the game's announcement was received. I had been wanting to see the exhibit there for a couple of weeks. I walked into the dome where images of previous Team GB successes were being projected all around. Almost in tears now as I write this, as I was then. It stirred every emotion within me. "I will be there," I whispered to myself.

I continued in my catering and temporary jobs for another couple of years. Frustrated that I wasn't using the skills I had gained other than helping a few friends out with injuries when something cropped up. By this point I was losing confidence in my ability to do what I had trained for. I took a supplementary qualification that enabled me to improve my massage skills and off the back of this, some much needed experience with a London based athletic squad.

During that course, my journey took me along the A12, passing the Olympic Park, I could see the venues being built and the progress being made. Although I'd temporarily forgotten about the little promise I'd made to myself in Trafalgar Square. However, at this point I was looking forward to making progress. I'd applied for the position of Resort Sports Therapist with a tour operator, and I was successful. I worked in Courchevel, France for the winter season. The following season I was again successful, this time working in St Anton, Austria. I had spent two winter seasons combining my love for winter sports and helping people move well, and continue to ski and snowboard.

That first season wasn't without its difficulties! It was just after the financial crash of 2008. The exchange rate was poor. And persuading people to part with their cash and have a treatment wasn't easy. Effectively, I was running my own business within a business. With no business experience at that time, I was thrown in at the deep end. What I was to learn in future years would have really helped me back then.

In 2010, the opportunity arrived to apply to be a Games Maker. My journey to London 2012 was on! I was selected, attended test events and training to learn about my role and everything I needed to know. I worked with some amazing people from different medical backgrounds. For me working at the London 2012 Olympic and Paralympic Games will be one of the most cherished memories of my life. And in 2016, I was to do it again in Rio de Janeiro.

**Rebuilding Me**
Fast forward to late 2017 following a business coaching event, I had excitedly drawn a plan of my future clinic. I was blissfully unaware of what was about to come. At Christmas time I had decided to take a proper break and not to work between Christmas and New Year, as I often had in previous years. But I spent nine days with ringing in my ears, which only went away when I was asleep or if I was speaking to someone. I was restless but at the same time I didn't want to do anything either.

My professional mentor put me in touch with someone who could guide me through some personal development. I embarked on some courses, which were going to shake me apart and then really help me rebuild. I realised how incredibly disconnected from myself I'd become. It felt like I had lost the essence of me and that I didn't know who I was anymore.

During this period, I shifted significantly, growing in ways that I had never considered. Each course brought a new and improved version of me. I learnt to accept the old versions of myself as part of me, while embracing the new, developing version. Letting go of many of my past troubles.

In one particular exercise, with the title: Self Love, Trust and Confidence. This question was posed at the start: what does a person who has self-love, trust and confidence look like?

A little voice inside, piped up and said, "me!" To start with I was having none of it! Didn't believe it, and certainly wasn't going to entertain the notion. But the little voice inside kept repeating itself at various points during the exercise, "me!" and a little later, "ME!" with a beaming smile from the inside. Over the next twenty minutes or so I gradually accepted that this had to be true and the answer to that question was in fact ME!

**Face Everything And Rise**
Fear is often written like this: False Evidence Appearing Real. But I also like this version: False *Expectations* Appearing Real. It's as if we predict a negative outcome of the pending event before we start.

Whichever version you prefer or is true for you, fear is only our safety mechanism to keep us safe and to protect us from real danger. However, it is a primal response that cannot distinguish between real danger that is going to cause us harm and something that is not. The question is, how do you respond to this?

Do you 'Face Everything And Run' or 'Face Everything And Rise?' It's your choice.

Do you remember that shy girl that I mentioned earlier? The one who wanted to hide behind the curtain, the one who wanted to blend in and go unnoticed. Only a few short months ago she spoke on stage, solo, presenting her very own content slot at Reign Like A Queen in December 2022. Let me hand it back to her to tell you how it went!

This was something I had never imagined myself doing until the opportunity was presented to us during the QIB Elevate Your Empire virtual event. I was inspired by Chloë Bisson's presentation, so I decided to apply and explore. Even though I thought that writing was my strong suit, something inside of me was telling me to speak. I am glad I did. The experience was amazing! I got to share some of my knowledge with the audience.

At first, I was excited by the idea of speaking. But as preparation for the event began, the thought of being on stage where everyone could see me, brought back all the memories from school. I had to face every one of those fears, what if I stutter or stammer? What if the words get stuck in my throat? What if... the questions kept coming, what am I doing? Can I really do this? One thing that helped build my confidence in the lead up to the event was my decision to join and contribute to the QIB Talk Sessions on Clubhouse. Clubhouse is a social media platform that just uses audio, it provided me with a virtual stage to practise on and become more accustomed to speaking to a different audience and being seen (virtually) and heard.

Just before setting foot on stage, I was quite nervous, my heart began to race, but I was excited too. "Breathe Christina, breathe!" I said to myself. Ironically this was the topic I had chosen to speak about and its incredible power and impact on our overall health. I channelled my skills and the confidence from my days as a gymnastics coach and decided I had to just go and be me on that stage. After just a few sticky words at the start, I found my flow and spoke from the heart.

When I came off the stage, I had this smile on my face, part of me couldn't quite believe what I'd just done and the rest of me was elated and absolutely chuffed to bits! Even gaining a compliment from the professional speaker who was next on stage. A side effect of choosing to speak at RLAQ 2022, was that the act of speaking on stage pushed me out of my comfort zone, helped increase my confidence and gave me another chance to grow.

Over time, I have come to realise that confidence is something that is built. We have to start small and remember that each step helps it to grow. Don't forget your setbacks and past experiences but learn from them. Everything you experience happens for a reason and is there to show you something. Practice helps improve confidence. Take steps each day to build yours. Not doing anything undermines your confidence. Look back at your previous experiences, what can you draw on or channel and bring into the present?

"From little acorns, grow mighty oaks" but it does not happen in one day!

Before I started writing this, I would have said that I wasn't really a confident person, that I felt I was lacking in confidence and within a few days I'd had to call myself out on my own BS! Because confidence jumped off the page in many different ways. But one of the most important things for me has been the reconnection to myself. Really understanding who I am and not defining myself by my qualifications or by what others think of me. Let me share a little secret with you, something that I often share with my clients. I ask them this question: where does health come from? And where does happiness come from? I hope your answer was, within. Because, just like health and happiness, confidence also comes from within. It starts with you.

From within these words I hope that you see confidence too. I hope that you see that the stories you tell about yourself are not always true. You are far more capable than you think.

## About Me

I am the Founder of Body Intelligence: Sports Therapy and Wellness Solutions. I'm on a mission to bring better movement health to the world. Having a passion for the fascinating human body, movement, health and wellbeing, it is my belief that health should not have to decline with age!

In my work, I seek to understand the body at a deeper level, helping people to resolve longstanding and complex injury, pain and movement issues by providing robust and sustainable solutions to the seemingly unsolvable. It's not about how you move. It's about how you are moving!

Since joining Queens In Business, the experience has been uplifting. Full of support and encouragement, this group of ladies cheer you on, celebrate your successes with you and pick you up when the chips are down.

In the last two years I have grown in so many ways. From the shy girl who didn't really want to be in the spotlight to the one who spoke on stage at Reign Like A Queen in December

2022, sharing my knowledge and how it can impact everyone's health.

I am so grateful to have had this opportunity to share some of my story with you and become a co-author. Something else I never would have thought I'd hear myself say.

This chapter is dedicated firstly to my professional mentor Simon Wellsted, who has stood beside me through every up and down over the past five years. Reshaping what I know about human movement. It is also dedicated to all of you who find inspiration from my words and take those first steps on their entrepreneurial journey. You are capable of more than you realise, keep moving forward!

# The Storm To The Calm

### Dr Irene Ching
Health & Wealth Coach

"Your success will be determined by your own confidence and fortitude" – Michelle Obama

*Trigger warning*[2]

My name is Dr Irene Ching and I am a family physician, property and business investor, speaker, money mindset coach and podcaster. I am a proud mother of two lovely boys and also a wife. Life is always busy for me and I run a tight ship with lots of things to accomplish and be responsible for.

I love my life and enjoy the excitement from my different roles especially when I meet new people. I run a few businesses and am especially busy with my seven-figure business. With help from management teams, I strive to accomplish my goals and serve more people. Giving service and helping others is what I like to do.

But it wasn't always like this. Previously, I was someone who lacked confidence, downplayed my abilities, hid away in my comfort zone and refused to venture out. I could not speak English properly and was so self-conscious when I spoke it, constantly worried about my accent, my grammar, my pronouns and never dared to voice my opinions. I was afraid

---
[2] Sexual abuse and eating disorder

that people would comment and criticise my grammar and imperfection. I was fearful of failures and often so afraid of changes and challenges. I hated interviews.

When I was younger, I was jealous of my brother and sisters because they were the favoured ones. I had very low self-esteem, felt rejected, depressed, and cried in the closets all the time, self-pitying with the opinion that I was ugly and selfish. How twisted my thinking was when I was younger. I cringe thinking about those days now – how I had suffered under the lies and mental blocks.

Over the years, I managed to get great results to get into medical school; God helped me to accomplish that which I am eternally grateful for. Studying in English was hard and needed a lot of work, especially subjects in medical school which were all new to me. I persevered and worked hard. But I was always made fun of by some lecturers who just liked to target me to give model answers.

I was so stressed that I had an eating disorder for many years. I felt the issue came about because I was no longer the top student in medical school and I lost my identity. I was dependent on my accomplishment to define myself. When I reflected on my eating disorder, I realised that I was trying to regain some sense of control. I experienced a lot of trauma through my childhood, having been sexually abused at six years old. The nightmares flooded into my mind daily.

On top of this, my sister was diagnosed with schizoaffective disorder at dental school and I blamed myself for not looking after her. I had to rely on God for His grace. But I was still relying on myself to seek His approval and to be good enough for Him. I felt I was not good enough and asked Him to love me more. Over the years, I slowly learnt about His love and His grace – that my identity is in Him. But it took a long time.

**Getting By Comfortably**
Despite my trauma, insecurities and secret eating disorder, I still took on leadership roles at university. But I had limiting beliefs that I was not good enough and not clever enough. I also had money blocks and shame.

For me, seeking money or earning more money meant I was not righteous. I believed that going after money was evil and that living poor was a good thing. I was afraid to tell people how much I earned. When I was offered more money for the work that I had done, I only charged a lower price. I felt that I did not deserve more money and deep down, I felt good when I was sacrificing and actually felt righteous when I lived below my means. I never wanted to show off.

So I chose family medicine as an easy way out so I did not need to do interviews even though I completed my examinations to be a specialist. I was afraid to challenge myself. I told myself that I had had enough of the grind and that family medicine would be good for my own family life. I had my two boys in those years.

I researched everything on breastfeeding, nutrition, sleep training, nurturing and early education. My boys were my world and they were very happy and content. They did very well for their 11 plus examinations – the selective process to be able to choose the best school.

Although I could see my boys growing and doing well, I was still not wanting to challenge myself and often felt like I wanted to stay in my comfort zone. I felt that I was not meant for more and that mediocrity is just right to get by. I did not want to fail and trying new things meant that I could fail. I did not want to be criticised by other people.

I knew that I was a good GP and that my patients were happy. I liked their compliments and gifts. I was a people pleaser. I felt that it was enough and that was it! But, deep down, I knew I was meant for more.

But then again, life was comfortable and living in my comfort zone was preferred. Why rock the boat?

**Awakening**

One day, my friend Andrew introduced me to meditation, spirituality and the quantum world. It opened my eyes like never before. I had an awakening and I knew that I had to go through this journey. It was a scary journey because I would have to leave my comfort zone and be challenged, be exposed to criticism and comments about my weaknesses and imperfections

I am not good enough, I am not good at English and writing, I cannot speak properly, I am not clever enough to teach, I am not rich enough to invest, I am too afraid to fail. I knew nothing. These were the limiting beliefs and blocks that I had to battle often.

I made the decision that my life would never be the same. I chose to choose myself and be the best version of myself. I only live once and I choose to live the best life and never go for second best. It is not a dress rehearsal. Life is real; I will shine and I will be courageous. Come what may, I will see life as happening *for* me and not *to* me. I am the designer of my life and the captain of my destiny.

I learnt so much about the quantum world and the power of the mind and imagination. I was hungry and continuously learning as well as eating good food for my thoughts and mind. I had to do this – nothing was going to hold me back.

I went through a lot of battles and obstacles along the way but these would become my story. I realised I could rewrite my story and that I decide how I am going to define my story and the meaning I give to it. My decision is to grow and to expand. If I stop growing then I am dying. Life is a gift, don't waste it.

I cherish every day – it is a blessing to be able to do what I am doing. I give thanks every day and I fill my heart with love and gratitude. That's how I am filled with powerful fuel to give and pour out to others. Love is the highest vibration and the most powerful energy. God is love. Life is beautiful no matter what is happening whether in the storm or in the calm, peaceful stream. I know that I am the tree planted by the river of life and love. Don't get me wrong, I am not perfect, I still have bad days. But I choose not to stay there. I choose how I feel about my situations. I choose to command things into being according to my faith. My ceiling has been elevated.

This journey is exciting and exhilarating. I still make mistakes and fail in my life so many times but I refuse to stop and give up. Changing my mindset and knowing the power of my mind and my spirit changed everything for me. I believed that God was for me and who could be against me? I can do all things through Christ who strengthens me.

**Positive Attracts Positive**
What does confidence mean to me? It is when you feel so self-assured that you know something well and are on top of your game.

Sometimes confidence can vary. It depends on our situations and the way we feel about ourselves, whether good or bad days and whether good situations or bad.

To illustrate, I met a man who was very confident in property investing, but not confident in the aspect of health and appearance. There was also an example of a woman who could run companies well, but froze at the thought of looking after young babies. She said she had no clue and was worried about how to carry the baby without dropping it . None of us are perfect and no one is equally qualified to do everything.

If you dig deeper, you will notice that those people who are confident, usually have these things in common: they believe that they are worthy and they value themselves no matter what situations they are in. This is what we dream to have.

Confidence comes from a healthy self-esteem and is our belief in our own abilities. Self-esteem is how we rate and regard ourselves overall and it is about how we see ourselves, no matter the situations. Self-esteem comes from the estimate of our own values. It does not depend on whether things are going well or not, or whether we know the subjects or not. When we have healthy and high self-esteem, even when things do not fall into place or go wrong, we do not then feel really bad about ourselves or blame ourselves out of proportion.

Low self-esteem is when we rate ourselves very negatively and believe in untrue things about ourselves. We think that we are unlovable, stupid, hopeless, unlikeable, no good for anything. Usually those who think/ believe those lies, live a tough life. It is extremely hard to live a confident life with these negative estimates about yourself.

Self-esteem and confidence are often moulded during childhood. It could be nurtured or undermined by the adults around us when we were young. When I was growing up, I had a very negative self-esteem. I felt rejected and not favoured. I put negative meanings to my life and focused on the negative things rather than giving thanks. From then on, I felt disempowered and I was crying all the time. The more I focused on the negative, the more negative things I attracted and the more negative things happened to me.

I was a child then, and of course, I did not know how the mind as well as the energy world worked when it came to the laws of the universe. I know about all these now. But thank God that I was saved in time and changed my trajectory at fourteen years old.

I was in a youth meeting and God spoke to me through this lady who was ministering. She told me five secrets only God would know. Rejection, low self-esteem and sexual abuse were mentioned and she said I had to give them to God and let Him sort them out. I was told that God loved me very much and I was crying uncontrollably. I was getting spiritual healing. I did not remember anything about the abuse. Then the image came back to me like a flashback. God said I would need healing and I had to forgive.

That's when my journey really started.

I came to learn that I am unique, special and one of a kind. There is no one like me.

I remembered years later, after I was helping my kids to understand their own values and worth, that I was still blinded by my own weakness. Deep down, I was asking God what I could do to make Him love me more. A performance mentality.

Then one day, God spoke through someone: that He had loved me to the maximum, He could not love me anymore. I just needed to receive His love and to learn to love myself. It was a revelation. Receive His love and to love myself and to value myself.

Just know that there is God that has put value and worth in you and that you are worthy and of value. You are unique. You are awesome. I remind myself daily of these affirmations that I am worthy and I am loved. Receive the love and then your cup will be full of love. Subsequently, you will be able to pour out love.

I submerge myself in love and I am grateful for all that I have. I give thanks every day. Gratitude is very powerful and it is a key thing to help you to have positive energy and vibrate at the highest energy level.

There are things to be done to build up our self-esteem. Self-esteem is also deemed as self-love or self-trust – it is not fixed and is not set in stone. It can be built, raised, honed and improved. It is your choice and do make it your goal to boost it. The mistake some people make is to look for self-esteem from the outside world. They crave admiration, praise, approval and compliments.

The same should be said about criticism and unkind words about ourselves too. They are all external factors and we should not let them affect our self-esteem. The pain would only last for a short period if our self-esteem is high. We should think of things and do the things that would raise it. Make it a conscious effort daily. These things include: doing what we say that we will do, being kind to ourselves, being truthful, being respectful and generous, being appreciative and grateful, choosing to not judge others, being productive and fulfilling our work as promised, listening to others especially those around us, and sticking to our boundaries.

Learning to say no is a very important skill to have. I was a 'yes' girl for a very long time until I burnt out trying to please everyone. I then learnt to say no and understood self-care and boundaries. We have to learn to say no in order to be able to say yes to ourselves. When we have enough fuel, love and self-care, only then can we help others. Just like the emergency video on an aeroplane – we have to put the oxygen mask on ourselves first before we can help others. If not, we are no good at helping others because we end up collapsing half way. We have to learn to ask ourselves, what do I need? To have a bit of 'me' time. I also find it useful to visualise myself being very confident to help myself in my passion to speak on stage and host my podcast.

**The Secret To Living**
I continue to work on my mindset and the power of my mind.

Over the years, my work balance has improved and I have been able to manage more things. My business grew and my property portfolio expanded. I also focused on money mindset because that was what I discovered plagued my progress. It was blocking me and holding me back. Once I worked on it, I had so many more profitable projects and deals open up to me.

I am here to encourage and persuade others to love themselves, to take on a journey of discovery and self-improvement. I love to coach. I have been through darkness and have seen the light and I want to help others. I know when I give to others, I am living my fulfilled life and that is my 'why'. The secret to living is giving. When I see others living their best version of themselves and living out their potential, I feel so fulfilled and happy.

How do you gain more confidence? Confidence is not something you are born with naturally, you have to work on it consistently. Everything around us is always changing and there can be a lot of uncertainties in our lives. But we need to focus on the things that we can control and that we can be certain of – not on the things we can't control.

The external world can throw curveballs at us, but we can choose to respond with things that we are certain of and what we can control. Having clarity with who we are and our intentions in life can help anchor us securely and give us confidence.

Be careful with who you spend your time and who you listen to. A lot of our identities are formed during childhood and we could be surprised at what we have stored subconsciously. Gain clarity and work on reversing any negative identity that does not serve you. Unconsciously, incongruence can shake our confidence. We need to live in alignment with our values, truth and integrity – then we learn to trust ourselves.

To be more confident in a particular field, skills or abilities, we need to continue to target and challenge ourselves in order to grow our competencies. Ask yourself, what can I do to improve myself today? Strike a balance – start now, perfect later. Don't be afraid of failure. Don't be halted by overthinking and procrastination. Just remember that small incremental changes consistently performed will create permanent and lasting results. Repeated actions and executions will gain capability.

And most of all, connect to yourself – make time to know you. Start with a good morning routine and chart out your day. Meditation is key! Affirm who you are – you can use 'I am' statements. Set your intentions. Visualise who you are. Share your feelings, thoughts, goals and your truth. But be careful with who you share them, not everyone will support you.

Remain vulnerable and expect to have stronger connections and relationships due to you being honest and authentic (no point having superficial relationships!). Remember to give, to contribute to others and offer help/service. The secret to living is giving.

## About Me

I am a medical practitioner who specialises in family medicine, wealth and life coaching. I am also a property and business investor, speaker, and podcast host of 'Be Happy, Healthy and Wealthy'.

A member of the Royal College of General Practitioners of London and member of the Royal College of Physicians of London for many years, I have several diplomas in family planning, women's health, diabetes and coaching.

I have a holistic approach to health and well-being and am passionate about human potential, helping people to reach their goals for happiness, health and wealth. I do this through my money mindset coaching programme, Quantum Wealth Creation Accelerator – an online course with weekly coaching helping you with emotional freedom, energy work NLP, intuition, superconscious mind and inner child healing.

I have helped my clients to be super money magnets and to live in abundance with ease and grace by healing their money blocks, shame and guilt. My motto is: Reset Your Mind, Reset Your Life.

In 2022, I was nominated for multiple awards including Best Speaker at Professional Speaker Academy, Speakers Award for Best Virtual Event, Newcomer Award, and Start Up Of The Year at Queens In Business Awards.

I would like to dedicate this chapter to my husband, two boys, and my parents. My husband is my loyal supporter and the love of my life who has sacrificed for me and my boys. My parents have showered me with love and financial support over the years despite having so many kids. I love you all.

# You Are Not Broken

## Dr Michelle Wyngaard
Founder
The Alchemy Academy

"The purpose of life is not just to be happy but to be authentic to your truth and create the life you want" – Michelle Wyngaard

I worked as a self-employed associate for twelve years with a dream of acquiring my dental practice to gain more control of my destiny and eventually have time and financial freedom. But unfortunately, it took me longer to take action due to a lack of confidence and self-belief.

I needed to know how to run a business and what bank would loan me that level of investment in the middle of a recession. On reflection, I wish I had done it sooner. The old mind chatter of the self-conscious (ego) says you will fail and make a fool of yourself. Stay safe and remain where you are, don't go out into the unknown if you are uncomfortable with uncertainty. It would be best if you had a business degree, all GOOP meaning — good opinion of other people implanted in my ego brain. I had to do much inner work to overcome this belief which afterwards I discovered was a false story I grew up with during childhood.

I finally took the plunge and did not give in to my fears because the thought of working for someone else was greater than the fear of uncertainty. I did it despite my fears. As humans, we are programmed to move towards pleasure or what's easy and away from pain (one pain was bigger than the other); I chose the pain for gain in the future. What was more frightening than uncertainty? I purchased a dental practice in the recession period of 2009 – I said it would toughen me up. If I could make it here, I could make it anywhere to withstand another storm.

I was right. I am facing the 2023 recession as I write this story. During the first six years in business, I was learning as I went along being the dentist and business owner, which is tough. Two identities in one – dealing with major HR staff issues and keeping cash flow afloat to pay the bills was by no means easy. Where was there space to enjoy being a dentist? Is this not what I came here to practise?

Over time my passion waned, and I resented being a dentist and a business owner. I lost my drive. My health suffered from poor diet, lack of sleep, and limited time for holidays as well as friends or family. What kept me going was the determination of my end result. That I was willing to go through the storm to achieve my WHY to time and financial freedom, to allow for the life I truly wanted – mentally, it knocked back my confidence.

I had to be strong because my family and employees relied on me. I realised I needed help from experts and coaches and connected to other like-minded business owners for support and encouragement. After investing in my first coach, I immersed myself in a six-year vortex of personal development.

**Overcoming Challenges**

The fear of not knowing and the uncertainty delayed me from just doing it and not being resourceful in my thinking.

Fear is a symptom of the mind wanting to keep us from harm. Therefore, we live in constant fight or flight mode as an adaptive response that can cause physiological damage mentally or physically. I choose not to live my life in this exhausting state; it takes the same energy to focus on a creative solution than on the problem we are facing. If you focus on issues, all you see are problems and get stuck in this holding pattern of thinking. We have free will to choose.

The best thing I did was to ask for help when I could not figure out my mistakes on my own by investing in various business coaches and mentors. There were occasions when I could not afford to hire a coach. I had to learn to overcome my emotional relationship with money to prevent patterns of self-sabotage. Now I respect my self-worth as a professional.

Confidence develops over time. Once you step into your new identity, it will show up as the latest version of you. So why wait? Just take small action steps towards your end result. Now I have shifted my identity to that of a more confident entrepreneur. I can do anything I set my mind to. I dance with fear and let it be my fuel for igniting the fire in me to transfer it into motion or action despite my obstacles.

My mentors and coaches showed me how to minimise mistakes, which affords me a shorter journey to success, highlighting the blind spots. It also allowed me to enjoy the entrepreneurial journey more and save money. I noticed the change in myself, developed more confidence, and put myself out there to be bolder and more courageous. Several of my colleagues and my patients commented on the shift in me. Choose a coach that aligns and resonates with you to accelerate your transformation and minimise the risks of navigating the minefield of becoming a successful entrepreneur or business owner.

Women need to remember to celebrate their small and big wins. My journey has taught me resilience through my mistakes and experiences. My confidence improved by accepting that failures are only feedback, not setbacks. I learnt to focus on what went well and what did not go well and that it's okay. There is always room for growth. The mistake is more valuable if you accept the lesson you learnt from it instead of pondering on it and giving energy to the failure itself. Change the meaning you give to your failures.

I discovered my hidden talent once I got out of my own way and realised I did not need the confidence in the first instance. It was a false story. I meet many females, both patients and colleagues, who say they need the confidence to follow their heart. So, I curiously ask women this one question: which of the two do they need first to do something they have never done before? Many answer confidence – it's courage. Confidence develops from taking the first step and looking back on your journey. You, by default, will then feel more confident.

I was seeking answers externally and could never find them when through my various coaching, I discovered that what I was seeking was already in me. So why seek validation from external sources? Introspection of your inner child shadow work also needs to be addressed. Acknowledge and embrace it to shed the old beliefs and ask for help from professionals to highlight growth areas.

How would I define confidence today? I give it a different meaning. Now I know better; I have to develop courage. Only then does it get easier; otherwise, we get stuck on needing confidence. The one thing that gave me confidence was relentless faith, belief that I could do it, and getting comfortable with uncertainty. If you are okay with that, then go into business. This is my new normal.

Once you can visualise the end result, you can create the plan. Everything starts with a thought with the motion to take action. We are all born creative beings.

When it does not make logical sense to the ego, I ask myself what I would love to do and why I want it and forget about the how for now. There is no secret to success other than taking consistent action.

I asked myself what was missing. This led me on a six-year journey of self-discovery and the evolution of my true identity. I took the plunge to write my story because six years ago, I was where you are, maybe right now – feeling not good enough, not perfect, not worthy, lacking confidence despite others seeing your potential. Perhaps you not believing in yourself and being fear-stricken about showing your truth.

**Self-Love, The Ego And Spirituality In Business**
Find the depth of connecting with your true self and develop unconditional love for yourself. How do I do this? In a world of negativity and chaos, we can lose our identity. Let your pain become your power, and use your wounds as wisdom and sadness as strength. This happens to fuel the change we seek.

First, we have to collapse our old beliefs and conditioning. It is a transformation process of identity shift and adapting to who we want to be without resistance to our authentic nature. We are all spiritual beings with various energy frequencies having a human experience. Today I find that the true spirit of the business owner is hidden behind the operational aspects of the business. We are overwhelmed with information and seeking more transformation. Heart-centred business connections are less transactional and more relational for long-term loyalty. People are looking for authenticity and simplicity, not complexity. You can redirect your focus and energy to approach life with a creative solution focus instead of being problem-focused. By looking in the mirror of life's reflections, refocus your energy away from the low-energy stuff in your life and use this same energy to create the life you choose to live instead. No matter what shows up for you, love yourself with your perfect imperfections.

The hardest thing is to be ourselves and stay aligned with our core values, true nature, and purpose. I became increasingly thirsty for knowledge about human behaviours. They say when the student is ready, the master appears. I sought in-depth answers to find fulfilment through investing in my first coach. I found myself at a crossroads of accepting that this void in my life was not going away until I faced it head-on and did some deep introspection. The more I discovered what was holding me back, the closer I was drawn towards what my heart and soul were attuned to following my life path of becoming a coach. Despite my successful career that was secure and gave me a comfortable lifestyle, my calling came to knock on my door louder and louder. *"Does my current profession make me fulfilled in what I really want?"* Many chase the lane of success and achievement without fulfilment, only to find they are still unhappy, just with a healthy bank account and an empty happiness account.

It was like a battle of the mind and heart, one saying accept the conditioned self and the other saying let go and evolve into who you were meant to be – my alter ego became uncomfortable with the thought of showing up as this new identity. But, on occasion, it wins the argument and reminds me of what it is to play small and safe. Finally, I am the captain of my ship, and now I take back control and get the ego to sit in the passenger seat. I am the driver of this choice.

On reflection, I realised that I was starting my awakening of evolving into the person I am today. However, it was awkward to admit that I did not recognise my old version any longer and felt uncomfortable wearing someone else's old coat that did not fit very well. So I started adapting to the new coat as it became more comfortable. I felt empowered!

The biggest part of life that holds us back is fear of failure, followed by success. Procrastination is a symptom of fear coming from the unconscious state.

Face the fear and do it anyway because everything you want is on the other side of fear. So it's important to take more action, stop overthinking, and just do it. I took a lesson from Richard Branson, who advises, "say yes now and figure out the rest later", as we tend to get stuck in the how.

Turn your fear into faith by

- Letting go of that which no longer serves you
- Get comfortable with uncertainty
- Stop playing small and safe – it gets you nowhere.
- Showing up as the best version of you
- There is no failure, just feedback

How do other people have confidence? They did not have confidence. By repeating their failures, they developed confidence – that's no secret.

The false sabotaging beliefs and events we picked up between the ages of three and seven from our environments are false. Developed along the way from various influences in our lives from school, parents and peers, which tend to play out as if it was in a movie with you being the co-star – become the main star in your own movie of life and stop living life to other people's expectations of you. Choose to live the end result of your true core nature.

Many women feel they lack confidence but are very competent in what they do. In contrast, some males act very confident but lack competence. As women, we can take a lesson from this. Anyway, who said we need confidence first before we need to do what we love?

The greatest lesson I have learnt through personal development is to start and not overthink whether I have the confidence to do what I desire. This is where faith comes in and lets the heart rule the mind; to avoid the conditioned mind from getting in the way of self-sabotaging our dreams and derailing our plans and goals. We learn to adapt to what our minds condition us to believe through life. Show me your authentic self, not the echo of your ego.

Through my journey of self-discovery, I stopped following and chasing the white rabbit, as my coach Peter Sage says –

when my inner voice asked that pivotal question, is this all there is to life? Of course, I could not answer at the time. Still, it left me baffled that after 40 years, I thought I had reached my optimal position in life; how many of us are happy in our careers, relationships, finances and health?

You can choose and create the life you want instead of being sucked into the world's issues. We all get different sets of cards to win this game of life. How you play is up to you. But first, we must overcome our limiting beliefs that undermine our courage to develop our confidence. Rivers never run in reverse. Let go of your past and focus on your future which is waiting for you. You can visit it occasionally but choose to live in the present. Instead, we become addicted to our old stories.

I had the greatest realisation of why we are all trying to fix our weaknesses, shortfalls, and parts we don't like about ourselves. My lightbulb moment came: I am not broken; there is nothing wrong with me or you – we go around in circles trying to find a solution for our brokenness, never finding a breakthrough for the long term. Here is the secret: you are not broken – you don't need to fix your problem with the lack of confidence you may have – to become what you desire. You don't need to go back on your past issues. Why waste your energy on fixing it when you can refocus your energy on creating the life you choose for no other reason just because that is what you want, without the resistance of needing to be confident?

This limiting belief keeps us in a limbo of making that leap of faith and just doing it. The self-conscious mind gets in the way, blocking what the superconscious mind wants to create. Years of the patterns of the unconscious mind are ingrained like a blueprint repeating behaviours that keep us safe. Our body vibrates energy at this familiar feeling, even if it does not serve our highest purpose. It knows no other way and is afraid to venture into the unknown because our mind thinks we are being chased by a lion the moment it has to step out of its routine of not being confident. Then, the fear sets off a roller coaster of old beliefs and why you should not do it.

I'm not worthy enough. Not good enough. Not capable. Not perfect.

Stop trying to repair yourself through various programs on how to do this and that instead. I now use my new modality to create the life I want. Ask yourself what do I want or love to create. If you want to explore more how a magnetic mindset can shift you from problem focus to solution focus without resistance and if it can help you shift those beliefs, I would be delighted to help you more.

We are born creators. We have what we seek already in us. So tap into your creative energy and notice what it feels like when life is flowing the way you want it to go and grow, and you will feel the glow.

Trust your gut instinct. It's your guide in knowing when something is right or out of alignment with your growth. We have to evolve as humans, or else we feel we wither and feel unfulfilled. We are here to fulfil our mission as a woman. We hold the code to solving many of the world's issues — we have this innate ability to have compassion and build communities. Find your greatness in whatever that is. Remain curious. Be open to being a student for life. We will never know it all and learn that whatever happens for me (victor mentality), not to me (victim mentality), I can change my perspective and know that how I respond to it is in my control – whatever happens externally is none of my business, so why give it your energy?

We waste energy trying to fix problems instead of creating the solution to design the life we want – it takes the same energy to do this, which is more fun than focusing on the problem – we all have a choice.

One lasting bit of advice, when you are at a roadblock regarding what to do, take these five steps:

1. Where am I now? (current reality)
2. What would I love to create? (desired reality)
3. Step into the emotion using all five senses
4. What's in the way or stopping you from taking action? ( reasons why you cannot )
5. Recode or change the meaning you give the resistance

Then ask, what is the next obvious step towards my desired reality? Then go do it. JUST DO IT! Remain open to all possibilities of what could be! Surrender in trusting the end result beyond our subconscious beliefs.

*Credit : The Work by Chris Duncan, Magnetic mindset 3 levels of consciousness : ego (conditioned) , unconscious (limited), superconscious (limitless)*

**Confidence Builders**
Get out of your own way. By that, I mean the ego (self-conscious mind). Learn to grow continually and contribute towards others by providing value upfront.

It's not about me. Take the focus away from you to diffuse the lack of confidence; otherwise, you feel anxious or fear sets in.

Be authentic to yourself even if your loved ones don't approve of the new identity you have chosen and created. When your heart and head align with your decision, go with it. Listen to your body and its signs of how you feel when something is not aligned with your true nature and purpose.

Remain curious and ask lots of questions to learn more about what fascinates you.

Give the word failure a new meaning – there is only feedback, not failure.

Create your direction in life from a conscious state by setting the intention with no tension or resistance. This is what I want to achieve with no tension – notice the old patterns and habits creating resistance to following your dreams and desires. Then take massive action to take the first small step in that direction.

Join a peer group of like-minded women or men that support your belief and hold you accountable for accomplishing your plans.

Most importantly, give yourself credit for how far you have come and celebrate little and big wins. Then, take a moment to reflect.

Self-care takes care of the weeds of the mind so that the dreams can blossom and avoid the false narrative of the mind chatter suffocating your dreams and hopes.

One of my coaches says practice makes it permanent, not perfect. Focus on mastering what you want to do to achieve a self-mastery level. By default, confidence must develop – many singers like Lady Gaga still need confidence before they go on stage; it did not stop them from becoming well-known artists, nor did Steve Jobs for Apple. Their passion overrides the fear of being judged, and they choose to create the life they want and the life of others .

What's in your way is a false narrative. We need to get out of our own way and move that dream into creative mode instead of focusing on the problem of how it is impossible to live a more fulfilling life.

In conclusion, I hope my story and transformation journey will inspire you to become a courageous, confident entrepreneur, step out of your comfort zone, and accept your truth.

There are many women capable of impacting the world to make a difference. What stops them is the belief that they need confidence first to create what they love to do. The evidence is out there, and I firmly believe that women hold the solution to solve and create a better world for future generations. To live in harmony with mother nature to form connected communities that build and not destroy the moral fibre of society.

To all that need to hear my story… I wish for you to find the meaning of unconditional love for yourself and towards others at the highest frequency of our emotions; love is at 528 Hz confidence is at 417 Hz.

Live in the present and appreciate and be grateful. Enjoy the NOW – if you still need to gain confidence, look at what you did not know a few years ago or borrow someone else's confidence in you. I believe in you, but you have to believe in yourself first.

## About Me

Born to South African parents, I immigrated from South Africa in 1999, seeking fulfilment in my chosen profession, following my graduation in 1997 in Cape Town.

I pursued a special interest in private cosmetic dentistry, which led to my passion for transforming patients' lives by enhancing their smiles. At the age of thirty-eight, I took the leap of faith to buy the practice I worked in as an associate dentist. After six years, I found myself burnt out as the owner of a four-surgery private practice acquiring the biggest challenge I faced: managing people.

Fast forward to the present, Dynamic Dental Studio is multi-nominated and received the best practice manager award for the south of East Anglia in the dentistry awards. I evolved into a multidimensional life strategist, using several coaching modalities, one of which creates powerful shifts within one session called the superconscious magnetic mindset. My career expands over 25 years has afforded me the experience to work with individuals and dental practice owners to amplify their communication, connection and confidence so they can make an influential impact in the dental world. I am passionate about mentoring, guiding my clients to effectively strengthen and elevate their personal and leadership vision to new heights.

Two times Amazon number one best-selling author, and professional public speaker, advocating holistic health and wellbeing. I was nominated by No.10 Downing street for services in dentistry for the Africa awards, recognised for services in supporting women in mental health and technical business support during the pandemic alongside other multi-award winning speaking events. I am also the Founder of The Alchemy Academy for dental business owners, a dental online coaching programme I am launching.

I dedicate this to my younger self to say thank you for the old version of me who got me to where I am today. I honour you with grace and gratitude, and I love you. To my family, close friends and colleagues, who supported me, you know who you are. You believed in me and saw my potential. However, I still had to take action. Your honest feedback was not my failure but areas of growth. I had to face my fears and do it. It was not about me but about who I was about to serve.

# Getting Visible With Confidence

## Paula Carnell
International Bee Expert & Speaker

"We must believe that we are gifted for something and that this thing must be attained" — Marie Curie

What advice would I give to my younger business self when faced with a problem, or stressful situation?

Sitting on the panel at Queens In Business' Reign Like A Queen event, I was asked this question along with three fellow panellists. Thankfully, the others answered before me, giving me time to really think about my answer.

I first started a business when I was 20. An artist that grew into a six-figure company with a greeting card publishing company supplying 700 shops across the UK, and exporting to 11 countries, then with a gallery, and finally, after 20 years, selling my own paintings for five-figure sums in London and the USA.

Over 30 years on, my mind could rustle up many a business crisis, or stressful situation. The first situation that came to mind was six years into my business, weeks after rustling up a 100% mortgage for an 11,000 sq foot commercial property, and discovering my husband was having an affair with my soon-to-be ex best friend.

I had decided to cast her from my life and keep the husband. Our marriage lasted another six years and produced two wonderful sons. I made the decision to stay as I believed that the bank manager wouldn't allow a single mother to have such a large business mortgage. If my older self had appeared and said, "Leave him, he'll do it again", or "Fight the banks, you can do it", I wouldn't have my two sons. No, despite the pain and trauma, I wouldn't change what happened.

Then I thought of the time, aged 40, laying on my sofa crying on the phone as I pulled out of the exhibition opportunity of a lifetime. I had spent the last three months bed bound, which continued then for a total of seven years with Ehlers Danlos Syndrome.

What advice would I give, knowing what I know now? Those seven years, when I lost my business, freedom, and health, I also learned about how to reconnect with my body, myself, my family, nature and eventually my new purpose. I needed the full seven years. The bees came into my life two years into that bed bound time.

Once I had recovered using herbal medicine and plant based minerals, I understood what was ailing the bees, why they were dying, and what needed to change in the beekeeping world, as well as the health and wellbeing of humans.

Interspersed in the first twenty years of my career were miscarriages, bad customers, difficult staff, cash flow issues, shareholders, property development, court cases, grief, menopause as well as great successes, winning competitions, achieving recognition, motherhood, and new relationships and respect for my work and what I was inspiring others to do.

By the time the mic came to me, I had a moment or two to breathe, and quietly ask the bees, what would I have liked my future older wiser self to appear and share?

Breathe. Kick your shoes off and walk out onto the grass. Smell the roses, fresh air, rain. Listen to the birds, and the buzz of the bees. Remember that we are all part of nature. Life is no accident, we each have a purpose, a reason for being. Step away from the hustle, the pushing, the fear. Embrace what your soul is crying out for, more joy, more connection, sharing of wisdom, serving others.

Once we slow down and reconnect, solutions come. We naturally attract those we need to heal ourselves, or that we can heal. Remembering why we are here, learning to live with the flow of life takes courage, and wisdom. These skills come with life, experience, pain, joy and love.

When I first started, my biggest fear was criticism of my opinions. I am aware that they are controversial as I am challenging conventional beliefs. But my faith that I am doing the work my soul is destined to do keeps me going. I believe it is your duty to share your message – withholding it could cause others to go through unnecessary harm or discomfort. Don't be selfish by keeping your wisdom to yourself!

Looking back at all the difficult things I have experienced, they each have become my special gifts. The challenges I lived through and survived, now all brought together to help me with my current life's purpose, to create a buzz about health.

My artistic background, the employing of staff, agents, exhibiting, speaking, are all useful skills in my current work as a bee consultant and honey sommelier. My vulnerabilities became my strengths. I have learned to run a business my way, more in the flow of the feminine, like the bees, more collaborative, and connected to natural forces. Perhaps if I had known that as a younger self, I may have reached this stage sooner?

I embrace the gifts of my traumas, the causes of every single silver hair, the loves and the losses that have created a fulfilling and joy filled life I am proud to feel is successful, with many years ahead. Should my future self have a message for me now, I'd like her to tell me, "Yes, keep going, you are connected, you do inspire, and you could go even slower, it's not a race."

The world right now needs a slower pace, and more people connected to the earth, nature, and each other. We each have a song inside us that needs to be sung. The melody could change, we don't have to sing the same song all our lives. I'd love to see more women embracing the challenges that being a woman brings. Rest when we need to, dance and laugh when we need that too, and of course the all important crying.

It's through the emotional scale that nature and our souls talk to us and guide us to what our work is and should be.

Right now the bees need me to 'create a buzz about health' and help more people see that we cannot be killing the bees without killing ourselves. If our environment is making the bees sick, and we are sharing that environment, then it's clear to me we HAVE to save the bees.

If I can help as many people as possible see that, and inspire a deeper connection to nature, and perhaps even bees and honey, then I know I have sung my song loud and clear and I am free to spend more days dancing barefoot on the grass!

## About Me

I work with organisations worldwide who want to work with bees and honey in a sustainable, naturopathic way, often thinking 'outside the box'. I first started my own business in 1990 as an artist, greeting card publisher and eventually ran my own gallery.

Exhibiting globally, my paintings sold for five figures. Then after 20 years I fell ill and became bed and wheelchair bound with Ehlers Danlos syndrome. During my 'cocoon' phase, my husband built me a beehive and bees moved in. Following a remarkable full recovery using herbal medicine and plant based minerals, I then reemerged 'creating a buzz about health', sharing the wisdom gained from bees and understanding the connection between our own health and theirs.

## Conclusion

Now we pass on the light to you. We hope that taking you through our unique paths inspires you to carve out your own, with your feet on the ground and your head held high. As you explore your vision for the future, let these powerful narratives guide you to move boldly towards your goals.

- Confidence is a choice and it starts from within
- Confidence is believing in yourself first, before anyone else, and carrying on that belief during challenging times
- Confidence is trusting your decisions without having to explain or justify your choices to others
- Confidence is accepting your flaws and loving yourself regardless of other people's judgements or thoughts
- Confidence is a muscle you have to train and nurture every day
- Confidence doesn't just show up when we succeed. We start to succeed when we are confident

And when you start nurturing your light from within, you'll notice how bright you can truly shine. When you start believing that you are capable, worthy, and secure, you'll notice that you can become your own catalyst of change.

It all starts with a single decision. The decision to embrace YOU.

# About Queens In Business

**Our Why**

Today female entrepreneurs are making waves in the world of business. There have never been more of us rising up, standing up for what we believe in and building our own vehicle for freedom.

It's our belief that each and every female entrepreneur has what it takes to be successful. Everyone has a gift inside of them, a skill or knowledge that could help someone who is struggling right now.

Female entrepreneurs have the ability to contribute to the world and deserve the opportunity to be successful, feel fulfilled and be visible within their business.

But the journey of entrepreneurship can be challenging at times and with just a fraction of women taking the leap to start their own businesses it can be a lonely ride. That's why we created Queens In Business.

Queens In Business is more than just a community. It's a movement created to recognise the achievements of female entrepreneurs, to support and guide them and give them the tools to increase their exposure in business.

Co-founded by five of us, it's the first of its kind, created by female entrepreneurs for female entrepreneurs:

Chloë Bisson – The Authority Queen
Carrie Griffiths – The Speaking Queen
Shim Ravalia – The Collaboration Queen
Sunna Coleman – The Writing Queen
Tanya Grant – The Branding Queen

Before starting QIB, we'd all built our own successful businesses, spent huge amounts of money on training and mentorship and invested years in growing our businesses.

We learned and mastered specific strategies and methods to get our businesses where they are today and we are now sharing those learnings and experiences with our clients.

Whether it is having a successful business or becoming financially independent, we aim to provide female entrepreneurs with the tools they need and a community to support them along the way.

**Our Methodology**
We believe that in business the ability to achieve success comes down to three core pillars:
- Education
- Empowerment
- Execution

Education for us means having the right skills, knowledge and strategies to achieve your goals and if you don't have them right now, having access to learn from experts that do.

Empowerment is about surrounding yourself with the right people to support you and cheer for you on the journey. It is about creating an empowering environment that nourishes you to be the best that you can be.

Execution means having the motivation, determination and drive to do what it takes to get to your end goal. Where we may struggle to find the motivation within ourselves, it's about having mentors to encourage you and giving you a kick up the bum when you need it.

At Queens In Business, we've created a powerful methodology that combines all three of the core pillars. We provide the hands-on business education from world class experts with the push you need to execute your strategies whilst surrounding you with supportive members to empower you to overcome any roadblocks that come up on the way.

**Our Mission**
We're on a mission to change the world of entrepreneurship. We want to create a movement that empowers female entrepreneurship and encourages their drive for success, not belittles it or judges them for putting their career first.

We want to eliminate the fear of judgement and the fear of failure. We want to create a world where it's okay to ask for help, it's okay to express your challenges and it's okay to make mistakes.

We want to support female entrepreneurs in becoming powerful role models for future generations who will believe in their abilities and believe they can achieve what they want.

It's our mission to provide support and exposure to Queens all over the world regardless of their age, background, or their position in their business.

It's time now for female entrepreneurs to rise up and be leaders, fight for what they want for themselves and for others, and get seen with confidence.

**To find out more about Queens In Business, go to:**
www.queensinbusinessclub.com

**Contact us on:**
team@queensinbusinessclub.com

Printed in Great Britain
by Amazon